The Bride's
Unique
Weddings

Sarah Ivens is the Deputy Editor of *OK!* magazine and has previously written for *Tatler*, *Marie Claire*, *Hello!*, *GQ*, the *Observer*, the *Daily Mail,* and the *Mirror*. She is married and lives in East London. This is her fourth book for Piatkus.

Also by the author:

A Modern Girl's Guide to Getting Hitched

A Modern Girl's Guide to Dynamic Dating

A Modern Girl's Guide to Etiquette

The Bride's Guide to
Unique
Weddings

SARAH IVENS

PIATKUS

௸ *Visit the Piatkus website!*

Piatkus publishes a wide range of bestselling fiction and
non-fiction, including books on health, mind body & spirit,
sex, self-help, cookery, biography and the paranormal.

If you want to:
- read descriptions of our popular titles
- buy our books over the internet
- take advantage of our special offers
- enter our monthly competition
- learn more about your favourite Piatkus authors

VISIT OUR WEBSITE AT: www.piatkus.co.uk

Copyright © 2005 by Sarah Ivens

First published in 2005 by
Piatkus Books Limited
5 Windmill Street
London WIT 2JA

e-mail: info@piatkus.co.uk

The moral right of the author has been asserted

*A catalogue record for this book is
available from the British Library*

ISBN 0 7499 2582 5

Edited by Jan Cutler
Illustrations by Megan Hess
Text design by Paul Saunders

This book has been printed on paper manufactured
with respect for the environment using wood from
managed sustainable resources

Printed and bound in Great Britain by Mackays Ltd, Chatham, Kent

Dedication

For my dad, Keith Ivens, who proudly walked
me down the aisle and has always been by my side
when it mattered most.

Contents

Acknowledgements

Heartfelt thanks, as always, have to go to my husband Stefan, who puts up with my mad ramblings and stressed afternoons. Love is blind, marriage is a real eye opener, but you've made me see life in Technicolor!

Thanks to Alice Davis, my fabulous editor – and everyone else at Piatkus, especially Judy, Jana and Paola. Thanks also to my agent, Ali Gunn at Curtis Brown.

Special shouts to: Deborah Arthurs, Jade Beer, Hayley Brown, Ben Buchanan, Andrea Cowell, Tara Demetriou, Julia Fairrie, Lucy Mines, Sarah Newton, Keeley Pitt-Jones, Sarah Pollard, Sue Shillum, Claire Steele, Rose St Louis, and the splendid Stapleford Park for providing inspiration.

Introduction

EVERY WEDDING DAY is special. The hours, weeks, months – sometimes years – of preparation ensures it will undoubtedly be the most memorable day of the bride and groom's life. She will look stunning in the carefully chosen dress, he will catch his breath as he turns to watch her approach from the end of the aisle, their family and friends will gather together, bursting with joy, laughter – and, hopefully, presents! And even though the lovely people at the weather office promised a clear day with lots of sunshine, no one – not even the ever-so-sensitive, anxiety-ridden, mother of the bride – will care when, despite a deal with the devil and lots of praying, the heavens open and it rains.

That's the thing about weddings: they are special. And although you may not feel like it now, as you're reading this book and embarking on a furious period of stress and saving, I promise that you will look back on the day you got hitched as the best day of your life. Without a doubt.

So why not make the day that you and your beloved tie the knot even more amazing? Why don't you really have some fun with it – make it memorable, fabulous,

glamorous, exhilarating, hilarious, unforgettable, sophisticated, exciting, phenomenal ... UNIQUE? Why not make it
one in a million?

Yes – that's right. Your wedding is the be all and end all
to you and your nearest and dearest, but think for a minute
about your guests. They may have been invited to a handful
of weddings in a matter of months, taking up many a sacred
weekend and mucho mullah (don't forget: paying for the
gift, the outfit and the accommodation – it costs people a
fair whack to attend). Should your guests really be forced to
sit through the same old, same old ...?

Will it really be the Wedding March and a boring
sermon? Followed by a slice of melon, lukewarm chicken in
white wine sauce and strawberry flan? Will the photos take
hours, and the 'cutting of the cake' look staged? Should the
DJ (wearing the obligatory snazzy waistcoat) really encourage the under-10s to fill the dance floor before you've had
your first dance by playing the 'Birdie Song'?

The answer to all of the above is No. You can make your
big day an exception to the boring-wedding rule! And you
know what the good thing is? It doesn't cost any more – or
take any more time – to have a charming wedding that
people will talk about for years to come. All it takes is a
little imagination, a tiny dash of bravery, and a massive
slurp of fun!

Now, I'm a wedding obsessive – I love the things. I loved
being a bride, and made sure our 300 guests loved being
with us. I love being a bridesmaid, a witness, a reader ...
goddamit, I even loved being the over-bearing tipsy school
friend who was so emotional by the speeches she told everyone she loved them (before wandering into the wrong toilet
and congratulating the father of the bride as he stood at the
urinal – I'm not joking).

So, why do I love weddings ... especially when my

husband and I easily rack up on averag
attend? Because my friends and family
inspired in their choice of food, venue, fl
and, of course, those special surprises tha
gasp in delight and give the couple son........ to gloat
about when they meet other honeymooners in their tropical
paradise of choice.

Researching this book, therefore, has been very enjoyable,
thanks to the remarkable talent of my wedding-planning
buddies and the weird-and-wonderful tips you can pick up
from any woman who has ever been a bride, as well as the
'how not tos' from any man who has ever been stuck at a
dreary do. I've also covered the basic rules and sensible tips
to make a solid foundation for you to plan from. You want
your wedding to be unique because of the entertainment, not
because there was only one toilet between 200 guests.

So start reading, and discover that getting married isn't
just about commitment, responsibility and love (you're an
intelligent girl, you know that already) ... it's also about
having the biggest party of your life, and enjoying every
second of it.

PS. Girls, a word of warning: you can't please all the
people all the time. So why bother? Some people – be they
friends, family or nosy onlookers – will find ways to criti-
cise and condemn whatever you decide to do. And some
weirdoes just don't enjoy weddings. Forget about them. The
day is about what you and your husband-to-be think is fun.
Put any rude remarks down to jealousy, stupidity or down-
right impoliteness, and promise that you will never be so
rude to a happy couple when they plan their wedding. The
people who love you will just be happy to share the event
with you!

What kind of wedding do you want? – the quiz

Ask yourself the following questions – the answers will reveal just where your bridal sensibilities lie:

1. You have a day off work. Ideally, how would you pass the hours?

   A. In the sun, on your back on a beach or in a park, eating ice cream.

   B. Catching up with friends and family.

   C. Going to the cinema, or an art gallery, or just eat toast in bed.

   D. Hitting the shops at opening time, then party till midnight.

2. You can't be bothered to cook, so you ring your local takeaway for …

   A. The works: an Indian meal for four – but just for you, and some Cobra beer.

   B. A healthyish Chinese, and call some mates to come and share it.

   C. Some information. It has just opened and it looks intriguing.

   D. The local taxi firm's phone number. Staying in is for wimps.

3. How would you describe your parents?

   A. They work too hard; they should chill out, take more holidays etc.

B. They're your lifeline; they're not just your parents, they're your mates.

C. Lovely; but you don't want to see them too often.

D. Disapproving; it's like they were never young.

4. You want to look beautiful for a big night out, so you ...

A. Wear your favourite dress – and some lip gloss.

B. Call your best friend and ask her for a makeover.

C. Experiment: you go shopping and get a haircut.

D. Decide to flash some flesh, and splash out on a designer handbag.

5. If you could go on holiday anywhere in the world, what would you do?

A. Stay for two weeks in an all-inclusive five-star hotel in the Maldives.

B. Hire a villa in the South of France with a group of mates.

C. Travel across Brazil and get to know the locals.

D. It has to be Los Angeles or New York for the shops and nightlife.

Mostly As – the Laidback Bride

Your unique wedding should cater towards your love of easy, stress-free fun. You would love a relaxed dress code, a ceremony in the open air, and perhaps even to write your own vows – or at least have some fun readings and some dancing. A buffet or BBQ would suit you and your equally chilled guests. You'll look stunning of course, but the groom won't get a shock as you approach up the aisle. Even on your wedding day, you want to look like the you he fell in love with.

Mostly Bs – the Sociable Bride

You don't think this wedding is *uniquely* about you. It's about your parents, friends, siblings, cousins – you want everyone to feel part of your planning. You'll welcome ideas from all sources – and will probably get some good advice, which you decide to accept. You are quite homely and traditional and will probably not venture far from home for the big day. The service at the local church and then a marquee in your parents' back garden sounds appealing, doesn't it? And maybe your clever harpist friend would perform during the meal.

Mostly Cs – the Adventurous Bride

Sod convention – you want drama! This really will be a unique wedding. Why get hitched the same way as thousands of others? You're full of imagination and not scared or embarrassed to go out on a limb, ask silly questions and risk good-spirited ridicule. You'll even stand up to your mother when she tries to tell you that a red wedding dress isn't a good idea. You want fireworks – literally. You want your friends to remember this wedding forever, so you spend over a year planning lots of surprises to take their breath away. Money may be an issue, but originality isn't.

Mostly Ds – the Glamorous Bride

This wedding will be unique – by local standards. You've seen the pictures of Catherine Zeta-Jones tying the knot with Michael Douglas in New York and you want the same. You put great emphasis on the flowers, cake, venue ... and your outfit. If you can invite only a handful of people, so be it. You want the most beautiful, elegant dress in the world and are prepared to cull the guest list for it. You will hire a professional hairdresser and make-up artist to come to your home on the morning of the wedding. Your bridesmaids are all aesthetically pleasing. The groomsmen's waistcoats will match the table decorations. You're hoping your big day will be featured in *Wedding and Home*. The honeymoon is incidental – you spent all the spare cash on diamanté shoes!

Chapter One

First things first

HOORAH – YOU'VE LANDED YOURSELF the man (or rather, he's lucky enough to have landed you!), he's presented you with a rock to make Alcatraz blush, and you've had that joyful few weeks of smiling inanely at strangers, flicking through glossy magazines and daydreaming during valuable office hours about what kind of dress you'll choose. Yippee – being a bride is fabulous.

Except, of course, that a bit too darn quickly things take a turn for the worse. You get fed up with smiling inanely at strangers, you've exhausted your newsagents of new magazines, your boss has told you off and you think you'll look fat in the dream dress. Not only that ... your groom-to-be is having panic attacks about just how much this is going to cost him, and your mother is asking to invite the neighbours – and the neighbours' children, and the neighbours' children's partners – none of whom you've ever met (but apparently your father and she had a good time at their BBQ last summer).

The boring bits

So, here is what I advise you to do. To stop yourself getting laden down with the arguments, the stress, the problems and the indecision that only a wedding can bring, make a plan early on and stick to it. In other words, get the boring stuff out of the way first – it's normally the duller, traditional stuff that families and friends get themselves wound up about. The sooner you've come to an agreement, negotiated your way to a happy middle ground, the better.

The things a bride-to-be needs to think of first include:

The date: things get booked up quickly, other friends will be getting married around the same time, people book holidays. Sort this out as soon as you can.

The guest list: OK, a few may come and a few may go, but you need to set the rules.

What you want: this is the most important thing, and you should not be outlandishly swayed.

What the groom wants: this is nearly as important as what you want, but not quite, as he really thinks weddings are a bit girlie/expensive/a lot of fuss about nothing, or all three.

Who is going to do what: don't rush into this, but start thinking about what you want your siblings, best friends and parents to do.

What you're going to do with your hair: oh yes, it seems like a vacuous point to add to your to-do list now, but if you've always dreamt of having a glamorous chignon in your natural colour, you'd better start growing out those layers and highlights, missy.

Do you want to lose weight? Personally, I've never seen an ugly bride and I think the shape that suits a woman best is her natural one – whether that be super slim, or sexy curvy … but if you do want to lose your spare tyre, do it sensibly. This means planning in advance and following a sensible eating and exercise plan. None of this last-minute crash-dieting, please, we don't want you fainting at the altar!

How do you compile a guest list?

Normal parties were never this tricky! Who to – and not to – invite to your wedding will probably cause you more arguments than anything else. Here are a few easy tips to help you get everything into perspective; after all, you can't invite everyone. Perhaps try inviting only those people who you have seen socially in the last six months (make exceptions for those who live abroad) or try inviting only those who have your home address (many casual acquaintances wouldn't – so how well do they know you?). You could be harsh and invite only those who sent you an engagement card, but then some people may have sent you a card only in the hope of receiving an invitation! What about inviting only those people who have met both the bride and groom – there's nothing worse than walking into your wedding breakfast and being greeted by a bunch a strangers? If money's an issue, explain and invite the minimum – then hold a house party when you get back from your honeymoon. If other people try to push you – that is, your parents and in-laws-to-be – be firm. It's your wedding and they should be your guests. Be fair though, you can understand why your father wants his best friend there; imagine your own daughter's wedding in 30 years' time ... you'd want your chief bridesmaid there to share your day, wouldn't you? If things get tricky, how about suggesting your parents and in-laws pay for their own guests while you pay for yours. That should make them think carefully about whether they really want to invite 'the nice couple who live next door'. Remember: the more people you have at your wedding, the less money there'll be to splash out on the unique elements.

How to control your parents and well-wishers

Ah, bless – people are kind. Unfortunately, however, other people's ideas of the perfect wedding may not be the same as yours. Put your foot down. It's harsh but the whole idea about having a unique wedding is that it's unique to you. Therefore, if you're an atheist with a love of the city, your friends are going to suspect something's up if you're forced to ship them all out to a country church to watch you say your vows by an over-domineering father.

Whenever you feel yourself getting weak, remember this is (fingers crossed) your one and only wedding. Your parents, your friends, your in-laws ... they've all had their own day to plan and stress over. Now it's your turn.

Perhaps, weaken on points you don't feel strongly about. I didn't care two hoots for what car I arrived at the church in, but my mother did. So she booked a very beautiful vintage limousine, which I was more than happy to be driven in. Give and take – as long as you're not giving to a point where you start to resent anyone. It has to be big smiles on the day, remember, not fisticuffs in the toilets.

When you're busy or tense, communicate via email. That way, well-wishers will still feel involved, but from a distance. You can decide how much you tell them, and they can't push you.

If things get tough, schedule a meeting, recount your problems and say a big 'Thanks but no thanks'. Blame your husband-to-be if needs be; he won't care – he just can't be bothered with another six months of you moaning about your mother.

When things have hit rock bottom with an interfering nag, hire an outsider. Get a wedding planner on your side and give him the reins. He or she is a professional; they can handle anything.

NB Are bossy-boots ever useful? Yes! It is your day, and you must do it your way, but other people have been there, done it and got the 'I was a Bridezilla once' T-shirt. OK, so 99 per cent of what they're suggesting is rubbish, but that one per cent may be top-tip fabulous. Don't dismiss everything just because they had it at their wedding. Unless your guest list is more than half the same as hers, borrow, cheat and steal her good ideas – she did the trial run on your behalf.

Money, money, money ...

... certainly isn't so funny, in a bride-to-be's world! Oh ya, the financial element can be a bit of a pain, especially when you really do want to invite the world and his mother, arrive at the church in a hot air balloon, and have tanned, muscular dancers serve cocktails to your guests while performing the hits of Broadway. Here's what to do:

1. Be realistic. If you can't afford to fly 100 people to Disneyland, you can't get married in Sleeping Beauty's castle. Not if you want those 100 people there, anyway.

2. Don't get into stupid debt. Yes, your wedding day is amazingly important, but so is buying a house, clearing your student loans, not blagging cash from your nearest and dearest, and getting a reputation as a tightwad.

3. Set up an account as soon as you can. And your future husband and you should have direct debits going into it every month from your other accounts, before you get the chance to spend all your disposable income on take-aways and shoes.

4. Find out who is helping financially. Hint like crazy until your families say how much they can put into the honey pot – you may be panicking for nothing, or be counting on a secret fund that just isn't there. Don't demand or ask rudely, but a few subtle comments should help them tell you.

5. Ask for discounts. Don't be afraid to say a product or service is just out of your price range. They may reduce it!

6. Shop around. Don't accept the first thing that comes your way. Yes, in general, people see an engaged couple

coming to them for something and they instantly double the price. So make sure you're not anyone's sucker!

7. DIY. More on this later, but think of your wedding as the chance to get creative – you'll enjoy it and it will save the wonga.

8. Call in favours. You can't imagine how many useful people you know. Could your friend with the beautiful handwriting draw your table plan? Would your colleague with the posh motor drive the bridesmaids to the service? Ask politely, it can't hurt. And if they say yes, make sure to thank them with a little token after the big day (a bottle of champagne or a bunch of flowers always goes down well).

So, money, arguments ... any other headaches?

Well, apart from attending a wedding the month before where the bride is wearing the same dress as you plan to, I think that's about it. Don't panic over small things. I've seen some brides go berserk at the following, and it spoilt the day for everyone:

◆ Rain.

◆ Snow.

◆ Traffic jams in the area.

◆ Father standing on her train as she walks down the aisle.

◆ Groom crying hysterically as he says his vows.

◆ Best man making rude jokes.

◆ Best man and chief bridesmaid snogging.

◆ Pubic hair in the wedding cake.

◆ Bride splitting dress while throwing the bouquet.

◆ Drunken guests vomiting in the gardens.

◆ Groom in the toilet for the first dance.

◆ Flies on the wedding cake.

Act with good grace. Let's face it, all these little dilemmas make your wedding unique. Have a laugh at your own expense.

The quickest way to make a wedding go with a bang is for the bride and groom to enjoy it. It flies by so fast. Expect the fights and the financial fallout, but when the day arrives, make the most of it. Perhaps even slip off somewhere with your groom for half an hour during the reception. No, not for some 'how's your father', but for a catch-up, for a chat, for a giggle about how clever you are for planning such a fabulous do.

KATE, 25

❝ My husband and I were staying in the hotel where the reception was being held. Halfway through dinner we sneaked off to the honeymoon suite – an intriguingly large gift box had been sent up there a few hours previously and we were desperate to see what it was. He unlocked the door – and it was mayhem ... in the best way! Our college friends had obviously found out about the room, blackmailed the key out of the reception staff and then gone mad with streamers, balloons, good-luck posters and a few bottles of champagne. And then, of course, we weren't as subtle as we thought, and the minute I started screaming and crying – with hilarity – they bundled us for a group hug from the cupboard they'd been hiding in! ❞

Now for the good stuff!

It's all very well saying your wedding will be a one-off, but where do you start? Where do you get the ideas from? Well, you made a good start with this book, because lots of amazing ideas will follow, but other places you can investigate further include:

◆ The Internet; go to Google and Yahoo and type in key words (wedding, marriage, nuptials with vows, readings, ideas, problems, menus, plans, flowers, food, venues).

◆ Magazines; these are great places to start. Visually, they can't be beaten. Rip out pictures that appeal to you, live with them for a while and show them to others. Pay as much attention to the adverts as to the editorial.

◆ Books; but don't just stick to the wedding variety. Expand your mind with good reads on etiquette, party planning, floristry, wine tasting, poetry, and fiction about getting married.

◆ Wedding planners; you're under no obligation to hire them on your first meeting, and even if they're too expensive/domineering, they may have some inspiring ideas or valuable words of warning.

◆ The venue; as soon as you've booked, investigate fully. Interview the head waiter, the bar manager, the patrons. Find out what's worked and what hasn't in the past.

◆ Past brides; trawl your memory box. When you've been a wedding guest, what did you love? What was naff? Phone the brides and grooms for useful contact numbers and advice.

◆ Your mother; sadly, she does know you best. She's the only other person who's as excited about the girlie details of this day as you are, so her research may have thrown up some good ideas too.

◆ Films; if you've always loved the fairground scene in *Grease*, or the ballroom extravaganza at the end of *Dirty Dancing*, copy it! So they had Hollywood budgets, beautiful people and a script, but you can pinch the ideas and ambience.

◆ Wedding shows; they are mayhem, but they are useful. You'll meet wedding suppliers, experts, other brides. Take your mum – she'll love it, and when she falls in love with the idea of a firework display, hopefully she'll offer to pay for it.

NB Never say never. Don't ever think you can't do it, or you don't have the imagination or the money ... or simply think it's not worth making the effort. It is. Everyone says it will be the best day of your life and you'll think they've gone mad. But it's true. It will be. If anything deserves your full attention, if your dreams will ever take flight, your wedding day is the day. If you can't afford to buy or you can't find everything you want, adapt, borrow, choose, experiment, bargain, make, barter, customise ...

The good wedding checklist

Before you get carried away on having an individual wedding to suit yourself and wow your social circle, do consider the following essential rules. They must be obeyed regardless of wedding style.

Top five wedding must-haves

1. Good – and plentiful – food provided throughout the day.

2. Decent – and flowing – drink, both alcoholic and non-alcoholic.

3. Entertainment; don't leave your guests bored for three hours while you go to have pictures taken and change outfits.

4. Friendliness; sit friends with friends, introduce people, dance with as many guests as you can, include all of your nearest and dearest in the speeches, and so on.

5. Music; you can never underestimate the effect of a bloody good DJ or band to put everyone in a happy mood, and make them stay until the bitter end.

CLAIRE, 29

❝ When I first started planning, I was at a loss. I'd never even held a dinner party before – let alone a party for 100 people. Then I saw a wedding fair advertised and decided to go along. Everything is in one place, and although there is an emphasis on the quick sell, if you know your own mind, you can use it as an idea factory. Hundreds of stalls are set out, filled with designers, florists, caterers, and so on. I picked up lots of free samples and leaflets and started to get an idea about what I wanted to do – and more importantly, how to do it well! ❞

Top five wedding must-nevers

1. Impose your views on others; make special arrangements for vegetarians, smokers, non-drinkers, children, your fighting, freshly divorced parents, and so on.

2. Refuse to have photos (and possibly a video); you'll regret it in the future.

3. Just think about yourself. It is your day, but thank people for travelling for you, dance with your dad, kiss your granny, tell your groom he looks great (everyone will be telling you how stunning you look and forgetting about him!).

4. Rely on the weather. Everything changes. Dramatically. Make provisions for every eventuality.

5. Drink too much before the service. Especially not port, which can give you a terrible headache (my cousin did this because her nerves were so bad and wished she hadn't!). The bride should stay sober to meet and greet and say her vows; hit the bubbly with dinner – and drink plenty of water. All that smiling and posing can really dehydrate a girl.

NB Talking of staying fresh and hydrated, a wedding planner gave me a great tip: pop a few of those traveller's dehydration tablets in your bridesmaid's purse. You can buy them from chemists, and my useful wedding planner says he's saved many a thirsty bride from a hellish headache with these terrific tabs.

Handy helpers

While you're busy planning the intricate details of your unique wedding, other people should be planning certain things.

The groom

Your groom should start to think about the honeymoon, and you both need to book time off work. He should also book wedding insurance in case of emergencies. He could think about the technical side of things, such as lighting, transport and the evening entertainment. Keep him involved – it is his wedding too, not just yours and your mother's!

The family

Your family should start coordinating distant relatives who need to book flights, trains or coaches, and who will also need somewhere to stay near the reception. His family should do the same for his gaggle. Let families know who is invited asap, so that they can look after their own broods – and not discuss it with people who won't be receiving an invitation. Your mother and mother-in-law will undoubtedly like to do something, so hand over some jolly chores that you're not too bothered about, such as finding the cake or the flowers.

The bridesmaids

Your bridesmaid, sister or best friend should be planning your unique hen night. With everything else on your plate, hand over the reins to a friend/sister/colleague you can trust, and who knows you well. As soon as you've set the wedding date, have a chat with 'the chosen one' about locations, themes, dates, and pass her a full list of contact details for everyone you want her to invite. This is also a good time to make a list of dos and don'ts. If you won't like it, put your foot down about strippers, trips abroad, and other girlie delights now. And just hope she pays attention.

Unconventional hen night ideas

If she's having a little trouble deciding what to do, leave this book open on this page next time she's over.

- Hire a cinema. Supermodel Liberty Ross hired the Rex Cinema in London for her hen night ... they watched chick flicks, drank cocktails, ate popcorn. What a cool idea. More and more cinemas are available for private hire now, and serve food and drinks to guests.

- Go to a spa. If the bride is worried about zits and dark circles, get some R&R with some luxury treatments, early nights and carrot juice. She'll thank you later.

- Throw a cocktail party. Long live *Sex and the City*! Get glammed up, serve canapés and down Cosmopolitans in vast quantities.

- Hit the road. Make an epic journey, her last as a single girl – be it driving across the Sahara Desert, California, or taking a barge around the pubs of the Norfolk Broads.

- Amsterdam. It's not just for the stags. It's a beautiful city with more than drugs and sex clubs – although they can be quite funny. So I'm told.

- Do fancy dress. Pick a theme and roam the streets, pubs and clubs of your hometown. What costumes? '70s and

'80s are always good (and easy), or try togas, bunny girls, LBDs (little black dresses), bad taste, Dallas v Dynasty, French maids, cowgirls, pyjamas, Hawaiian hula girls, policewomen, nurses ... the bride will certainly get lots of (wanted and unwanted) attention, and free drinks!

◆ A day at the races. Get all *My Fair Lady*, drink Pimms and have a flutter.

◆ Hire the wedding venue for a super-long, tasty lunch – she'll think this is very thoughtful, then present her with a slide show or photo album of her life, the groom's life ... and their life together.

◆ Do a slumber party – but all wear wedding dresses (search in charity shops, or get your old one out!). Watch *Father of the Bride, Four Weddings and a Funeral* (all the tear-jerkers) and toast each other with champagne.

◆ Hire a villa somewhere hot. Relax, read, gossip, dance, laugh – and get a healthy glow for the big day.

NB Don't make your hen night too outrageously decadent! If it's too pricey some friends may not be able to afford to join you. And think twice about asking people to book days off work to celebrate – their holiday allowance may be minimal.

Don't think hen nights have to be debauched, drunken disasters. Most girls just love the excuse to get together without their husbands and boyfriends, and act like teenagers again: gossip, learn dance routines, have food fights, flirt, and so on. Thank your mates for coming to your hen do with little pressies – yes, chocolate willies are fun, but even nicer are bath oils, frilly knickers, sunglasses, and even little notes simply expressing your gratitude, with a picture of you all together when you were younger.

CAROLYN, 30

❛ I felt too stressed and mature to do the whole out-and-loud week in the Balearics for my hen celebrations. I was finding planning the wedding – and dealing with my parents and in-laws – so all-consuming I wanted to limit the hen thing to one day. And I was four months pregnant so I couldn't drink. I really felt pity for my bridesmaid having to plan something fun for me – because I wasn't feeling much fun. But she was great, she organised for eight of us to travel first class on Eurostar and have lunch at one of Paris's best restaurants. Then we shopped for an hour before returning. I was in bed by 11.00 p.m. and happy. It was the perfect balance. ❜

Secrets of Success

◆ Start the uniqueness early by celebrating your engagement in style. An 'I've got a rock on my third finger!' party doesn't need to be as formal as a wedding, so you can really have fun. Throw a rave in your back garden, build a bar and have a retro disco, hire your favourite hang-out and fill it with friends and balloons.

◆ If your groom-to-be didn't present you with the ring, choose it together and don't feel limited to the typical diamond solitaire if you want to be more original. Ask a jeweller to design something unique for you (you can then get the wedding band designed to fit it, too) and dabble with stones and metals. Just remember: hopefully you'll be wearing it forever, so you need to think carefully if stepping away from the traditional. It's very popular at the moment to go for a pink or purple diamond.

◆ A recent, very cool trend for modern brides is to send a 'save the date' reminder before – or, for a laidback wedding, instead of – the actual invitation. Friends of mine sent magnets out in their Christmas cards six months before the big day. Perfect. It reminded everyone they had something to look forward to, and it looked great on my fridge.

◆ Other couples choose to inform everyone that they've booked the date by sending simple postcards of where they will be tying the knot.

◆ More fab ideas include getting the date printed on packets of loveheart sweets (Kate Moss had these at her 30th birthday party), posting a caricature card of the pair of you with a witty message, or recording CDs with your first dance song and a spoken message about your engagement and forthcoming wedding on it. Look on the Internet for details of how to do all these fun things.

◆ Start practising your royal wave and smiling inanely all day. Your hand will ache, your face will ache – that's a given – but a little strength training may help.

◆ As soon as you start thinking of dresses, flowers and menus, get a wedding file – this will not only help you formulate your thoughts but it will also be a great keepsake for you (or a thank-you present for your mother).

◆ When it comes to asking your nearest and dearest to play a special role in your wedding, don't feel constrained by tradition or finances: if you have to ask your ten best friends to be bridesmaids to avoid hurt feelings, then do it. What's the price of a dress compared to a mate's happiness? Nothing. The same goes for men; who said a groom couldn't have four best men?

♦ Also, when handing out responsibilities, don't feel constrained by gender. If your best friend is a bloke – make him the male equivalent of your chief bridesmaid. Kate Moss and Sadie Frost were joint best women at a male friend's wedding and donned stylish grey suits and waistcoats. It's only a little twist on tradition, but it makes it unique.

♦ It seems a long way off, but the moment you walk up the aisle is very nerve-wracking – make sure you're doing it with someone supportive and loving, be it your father, step-dad, an uncle or a brother. Some unique brides walk up with their beloved canine friends! Another girl I know, who lost her father shortly before her big day, chose to walk in with her husband-to-be. He, after all, was the most supportive, loving man in her life.

♦ When you're planning your uniquely fabulous day, don't lose all sense of realism. A few memorable show-stoppers are cool; overdo it and you'll look cheesy, twee or egocentric.

♦ Remember hens: you don't have to be girlie, girlie on your night out. Play the men at their own game: take golf lessons, go go-karting or paint-balling. You could even go camping and do outdoor pursuits such as clay pigeon shooting.

♦ If you don't want to waste a weekend being sick in the gutter, use your hen night to learn some cool, new skills. My friends and I had line-dancing tutorials on my hen weekend and we laughed until we cried – and learnt some moves for the nightclub that evening. Also try cocktail-mixing lessons, ballroom dancing, erotic dancing or watercolours – if you want to relax.

Chapter Two

Location, location, location

WHERE YOU DECIDE TO HOLD your wedding will say more about your uniquely brilliant planning than anything else. As soon as the invitation drops on your guest's doormat, the anticipation begins: who will be there, what will the bride be wearing, will there be a disco ... and, wow, you're holding the big day there? How cool.

When you're choosing a memorable location, remember the following rules:

1. Don't put uniqueness above suitability. Yes, you can now hold scuba weddings, but who could/would/should go

underwater with you? Be memorable, but don't be weird if it means no one can make it.

2. Cost. If you want to hold your wedding somewhere ridiculously cool, you should pay for it; don't burden your guests. Yes, get married in Las Vegas if you want to, but don't get the hump when people turn your invite down, and perhaps you could share the hotel costs with those who do decide to splash out.

3. You may want to go 'way out' with your wedding venue, but make sure your partner feels comfortable about it, too. Yes, the bride makes most of the decisions, but such a big thing should be discussed equally.

4. A Bedouin wedding in the desert sounds exotic, but all venues should have basic things to make your guests feel comfortable, such as toilets, washing facilities, cool drinks, somewhere to keep food at the right temperature and confirmed transport links. (Even if you have to lay it all on yourself, make sure it's organised.)

5. Don't go all out for cool above fun – you want your guests to have a great time. You want them to dance until dawn and laugh and smile, and they'll only do this if they feel comfortable. Don't hire an R'n'B disco in a Soho members' club if your family and friends will just gawp and grumble all night. Think of your market.

The world is your oyster

Having said all the above, options for inventive brides really are limitless. Restrictions about where and how you get married have been removed, and couples can now look all around the world for their perfect venue. When you're looking for somewhere, start with a general idea of what you're after:

1. Are you holding the ceremony in a church or having a civil ceremony?

2. What do you need/expect the weather to be like?

3. Do you want the food and drink to be a priority?

4. Would you ideally like the ceremony and reception to be within walking distance of each other?

5. Do you want to hold the wedding near to your home or your parents' home, or are you not bothered?

6. Is it suitable for children, the elderly or the disabled?

7. Is it too big or small? If you've got only 50 guests, having dinner in a large hall will restrict the atmosphere.

When you have satisfactory answers to the above, start looking as quickly as possible to avoid disappointment, and then, when you've paid your deposit (expect to pay 50 per cent when you book), get everything in writing. This is the biggest party you'll ever throw; you don't need the hassle of worrying that things could go wrong. Now might also be the time to sort out wedding insurance.

NB If you've always dreamt of holding your wedding at a five-star hotel but imagined it would be too expensive, strike a deal with the coordinators. If you can guarantee that a certain number of rooms will be reserved by your guests, they may throw in the cost of the honeymoon suite, the canapés or the room hire. If you don't ask, you don't get.

Church weddings

If you want to get married in a church, you don't have to settle for the nearest one to you or your parents. If you've had your heart set on a beautiful chapel in the countryside, go to see the vicar or priest and introduce yourself. Ask how you could make your dream come true. Most churches welcome wedding services to raise money, awareness and visitors, so will offer to marry you if you fulfil some basic requirements. You may have to attend bible classes, marriage lessons, church every Sunday – or a more lenient vicar may be happy just to see you at Christmas and Easter.

The media always say that religious ceremonies are out of favour, but don't believe it – if you like the look of a church, lots of other couples will too. Book as soon as possible. If another couple is getting married in your chosen church the same day as you, ask for their contact details as soon as possible, so that you can discuss flowers and colours – this will save you money and stress!

When you're booking a church, check the number of seats, if confetti can be thrown, if there is a choir and bell-ringers, if the ceremony can be photographed and videoed, if guests can take mass, and what the parking is like.

> ## OTHER FAITHS
>
> Wedding ceremonies in all religions are more rigorous and formulaic than a civil service, but whatever your beliefs, your wedding service will stand out by including music, colour and atmosphere. Ask talented friends to decorate the temple, synagogue or mosque with imaginative displays of flowers and swathes of fabric. Speak to the person performing the service to see how far the rules and tradition of your religion can be pushed.

If you're not going religious

Thousands of new places get their wedding licence each year, so lots of places now double as venues to have the service and reception afterwards. Also, think about the ideas below – check with your favourite one of the following to make sure it's licensed:

◆ Football stadiums; to keep the groom happy.

◆ Golf, cricket and tennis clubs, or decent, reasonably priced clubhouses; you can even hold it at a famous place like Wentworth or Wimbledon.

◆ Hotels; investigate the ballrooms, drawing rooms, gardens and libraries for an all-in, easy wedding venue.

◆ Private homes; for a personal, intimate day.

◆ Landmarks; get married on the London Eye, Tower Bridge, at the Blackpool Tower, Bath Pump Rooms, for example.

- Gardens; exchange your vows in an orchard, next to a lake, in the open air, or even at the botanical gardens at Kew in London.

- Zoos; get animal with the animals.

- Theme parks; some have licences for white-knuckle weddings.

- Universities; get married at your old stomping ground.

- Museums and art galleries; traditional settings without religion, and artefacts to amuse the guests during the line-up. Serve champers while guests mingle with dinosaurs at the National History Museum.

- Town halls; the classic confetti shot on the steps is a winner.

- Where did your parents get hitched? Go back to the future (if it still exists and isn't too grim).

- River ceremonies; tie the knot cruising the Thames, or go further afield.

- Apply for a licence for your house, or a friend or family member's, and put up a marquee and portable loos.

- School's cool; if your old school (or one you've always admired) has a chapel, the chances are you can marry there. Just check the rules.

- Racecourses; perfect for Pimms and fresh air.

- Film studios; Pinewood, Shepperton, Universal and Disney resorts all host wedding ceremonies and parties now.

- Castles and stately homes: for a purely romantic, wow factor; infamous houses like Longleat and Clivedon are now available.

ELLA, 35

❝ We tied the knot at Stapleford, a beautiful country house in Leicestershire that has been transformed into a hotel – but it's more than just that. There are private cottages on the grounds that the girls stayed in the night before, while the groom and ushers stayed in the main house. In the morning, we went to the spa while they played golf, before moving on to the orangery for the ceremony. Afterwards we served champagne as guests wandered in the grounds, playing croquet, giant chess and watching falconry displays. My favourite picture is of me and my new husband with an owl called Bernard sitting on my arm! The whole wedding was traditionally beautiful but uniquely relaxed – there were no set times or restrictions, we just wanted our guests to relax and have fun. ❞

If you're looking for somewhere to hold the party

◆ Film or television sets; imagine getting married in Albert Square or on Coronation Street.

◆ A casino restaurant; dinner and drinks before having a flutter.

◆ A street party; just make sure you get on with your neighbours.

◆ In your favourite restaurant.

◆ At an ice rink or roller disco.

◆ Go to the place where they make your favourite food or drink – Cadbury's World, Cheddar Gorge, a vineyard or orchard.

- It sounds fishy, but an aquarium is very cool.

- Nightclubs will have great light and sound systems.

- Your local pub – why not? The landlord's your mate, the beer is cheap, it's near your house ... what's not to like?

NB If your venue is difficult to find, enclose a map and directions – and don't think these have to be dull. Instruct a local calligrapher, artist or designer to make your own commemorative guide. Draw little extras, such as picking out the local spot where you first kissed, went to school or where your current home is.

Sun, sea and stress-free weddings

The ultimate location for the modern, adventurous bride is to get married abroad. However, it does mean that some people won't be able to afford – or want – to travel, and you will have to give plenty of notice, but once you're there, how wonderful it will be! You can make the day uniquely yours ... it won't be compared to other friends' weddings because if you pick somewhere carefully enough people won't have been there before.

When planning a wedding abroad:

1. Go onto every website you can find.

2. Telephone tourist boards and embassies for local information.

3. Never get married somewhere without going there, or being recommended by someone you can trust.

4. Be sensible. If you burn like a lobster, don't go for a beach wedding at midday.

5. Check local public holidays and whether any strikes are likely.

6. Learn the lingo – only a few words, just enough so that you will be treated well.

7. When you've picked the hotel, tell them it's your wedding! Don't just book the service at a local church, and not tell the place where you're staying. You should expect flowers/fruit and champagne in the room, and special service as well as the most romantic of restaurant tables at all times.

8. If you're staying on for your honeymoon, make sure you get rid of the relatives. You don't want to bump into your in-laws as you're enjoying your first sunset as a married couple. Move on to an even more decadent hotel.

Even if you are marrying abroad, ask your hotel and the locals and you may be able to locate a fellow national who's a vicar to perform a blessing. Friends of mine held a fabulous wedding in Provence, and the finishing touch was having an English parson perform the ceremony – it meant that everyone felt a little at home in the middle of France.

If you're getting married in a foreign country, present your guests with a language guidebook in their welcome pack or as a wedding favour. Make the most of local arts and crafts when getting hitched abroad, and present your guests with a gift that will always remind them of the special place you chose to marry in (and make sure it is carefully wrapped for travelling home).

NB If you're getting married in the sun, the obvious choice is to get married on the beach – and what could be nicer? Just make sure there is protection from unexpected wind and rain, an easy walkway, and that you can hear everyone. Also make sure your guests have got adequate sun protection and water.

The boring bits of getting married abroad

1. Verify what documentation you need and how long you need to be in the country before a ceremony can legally take place.

2. Sounds obvious, but don't do a Jerry Hall when she married Mick Jagger – check that exchanging your vows in another country has legal weight in your own country.

3. Ask your doctor what vaccinations you need, and inform your guests. Make sure everyone has finished any required medication (such as malaria pills) before the wedding day.

4. Find out from the embassy how long it takes to complete documentation, and if they know of any previous hiccups when people from your country have married there.

NICOLA, 30

❝ When my Greek Cypriot boyfriend and I got engaged, everyone expected that they'd have to travel from one country or the other for a middle-of-the-road wedding which encompassed both our family traditions and country's quirks. But we decided to take a risk – and thankfully it paid off. Costas's family flew in from Cyprus, and we made them feel at home by holding an all-singing, all-dancing Greek Cypriot wedding – with all the traditional food and music, as well as pinning money on my dress – in London. Then, instead of having a honeymoon, we flew with our closest friends and family to Costas's parents' village, where we drank beer, ate sausages and mash and danced to the Beatles. My dad taught Cockney rhyming slang to the locals and had the time of his life. 🍢

Instant impact

Your wedding can stand out a mile from the minute your guests look at a map, with a little careful thought:

Flash mobbing

Now, some people don't plan their weddings for months, or they want to play things a little bit cooler and leave their guests guessing until the last minute. This is where flash mobbing comes in – it means keeping the location a secret, and then texting your friends and family an hour or two before kick off. Give them warning of the date and dress code, and then let the rest be a surprise. Think Britney Spears. You don't even have to tell them that they'll be attending your wedding – you can just say it's a special event. If you do decide to do this, pick a location that is easily accessible by public transport, and don't get annoyed if people can't make it there in time, if at all. It's your choice to be this radical! But it will make an impact. This is very celebrity cool – Hollywood stars are always keeping their weddings a secret, before notifying family a few hours in advance to keep the media away.

Stunning scenery

An important thing to remember is the initial impact the venue will have as your guests arrive. You want them to think, 'Wow, this is beautiful!' or at least, 'This looks like a place where I could have a lot of fun.' When you and your partner are inspecting locations for your big day, think carefully – and ask questions:

1. Behind the rose garden, is there a sewage plant?

2. Can you hear a motorway or train line from the reception area?

3. Are the gardens stunning but the inside boring – or vice versa?

4. If, God forbid, it rains and you can't use the gardens, is there a suitable overflow room for damp guests?

5. Are there any building works planned?

6. Will the venue be getting painted and the gardens pruned before your big day?

7. Will you be allowed to brighten up the area with your own plants, trees and decorations?

And lastly, take your parents and well-chosen friends along and observe their initial reactions. If they smile a lot, it's a goer!

JILL, 35

❝ We fell in love with a register office in our town centre – the building was 200 years old, and there was a grand, sweeping staircase I'd have to descend as Mrs Martin. The interior was perfect – and convenient – but I was a little worried about the plain, greyness of the exterior. So I checked with the council, and then contacted a landscape gardener, who allowed us to hire a dozen or so aluminium pots, which he filled with lavender. We placed these on the steps to the register office and because it was a hot day, the fragrance filled the air as our guests walked in. So if you're venue doesn't have a good garden, buy one! ❞

Lush lighting

A good idea would be to visit your chosen location on a number of different occasions, at all times of the day. And if you have time the year before, do a recce on the same month as you intend to hold your wedding. You want to make sure, for example, that the venue doesn't look cold, dark and gloomy on a dark winter evening. Also, for a summer ceremony, you need to make sure that on a hot day there is a little area of protection from the heat and that your guests won't be blinded during the ceremony under a glass roof. And remember: if you want an intimate, subdued wedding with candles, don't choose July!

Upstairs downstairs

Don't feel bad about reviewing the staff – after all, if you want to create an atmosphere of old-school sophistication, having a herd of hungover 16-year olds in charge of silver service may diminish the elegance. You are completely within your rights to interview the reception manager and the head waitress. If you want experienced waiting staff, say so. If you want them to wear clean, suitable clothes, say so.

Perhaps sort out an agreement with the venue. Set a clause that states if anything goes wrong at your wedding due to the staff's incompetence, you will receive a discount. This should limit the excuses of staff shortages, staff lateness or leaving early, unclean toilets, unmanned cloakrooms, and so on. You want your wedding to be unique … but for the right reasons. The staff at your venue is the oil that allows your wedding wheel to turn smoothly.

If you have more than 100 guests, don't consider hosting a sit-down meal without employing a master of ceremonies. He will organise the timing of different courses, make sure the speeches are listened to and keep the line-up waiting time to a minimum. If you want something a bit different, ask a good (loud and bossy) friend to be the master of ceremonies. Or hire a town crier, complete with red coat and brass buttons. Or employ a poet, who can rhyme his way through each instruction. Or if your father-in-law is loud and proud, why not ask him to do the honours; your dad's doing a speech, give dad-in-law a role, too.

INSPECTOR CLUE-SO?

If you live nearby, sneak about your chosen venue while they are holding another wedding before you put down your deposit. Don't stalk the bride and groom, but just peer in through a few windows, hang about the car park, or linger in the gardens. Yes, you'll look weird, but brides are known for their neurotic behaviour, so who cares? Make sure everything looks like it's running efficiently, and you may even get a few ideas about what decorations or layout looks good.

If the venue is a hotel, inspect the bedrooms. Before you recommend your nearest and dearest to stay there, it's only right to check that the rooms are clean, private and have all the must-have facilities.

Size matters

You may have fallen in love with an orangery on a hill, but if it holds only 20 people and you've got a large family with 40 cousins, it's not the place for you. To help you find a suitably sized venue, physically sit and count all the spaces in a ceremony venue to make sure everyone will get a seat. Then, at the reception venue, decide how many tables you will need (and how many people you want to sit at each table), and then ask the venue to lay the correct number out. This will allow you to see how much room there will be for the waiters to move between the tables, as well as the guests' access to the bar and toilets, and how much space there will be left for a dance floor and DJ.

NB As soon as you're engaged, check out every venue you get invited to. Pay special attention to other people's weddings, party venues and restaurants, to analyse what you like and dislike. And think about what you could add (or get rid of) when you do choose your perfect location.

On the move

How do you get your guests from the service venue to the reception?

If it's near enough, it's lovely to walk. You can get some fresh air and catch up with friends and it's a great opportunity for the photographer to get some natural pictures. If the weather looks a bit dodgy, send a sensible usher out on the morning to stock up on those massive golf umbrellas. I've even seen a bride in wellies and the effect was charming. Another bride I know travelled to the service on horseback, which was very brave considering she was in full wedding regalia and it was raining. But it made an impact – and the horse even wore a matching veil! Stella McCartney travelled to her Scottish wedding on a horse and cart.

If you have a little further to travel

◆ Hire London taxis for the main party, and get the rest of the congregation in a big red bus. Make it open-topped if you've got a July or August wedding, and serve drinks on board. If you want everyone to be silly by the time they arrive, make sure the driver is equipped with some top tunes.

◆ Indulge your new husband's love of motors and hire a vintage car. Decorate it with ribbon and ask an usher to place a bottle of champagne on the back seat for your trip from the ceremony to the reception.

◆ Rent a character car. If your dad loves *Only Fools and Horses*, pay to go to the ceremony in one of Del Boy's bright yellow Reliant Robins. Sweep your bridesmaids off in the Pink Ladies' car from *Grease*. Impress your fiancé by arriving in one of James Bond's Aston Martins.

All of these – and more – are available to hire through the Internet.

◆ Get a taste of the Orient and arrive on a rickshaw.

◆ For old times' sake, ask your dad to drive you in the family car.

◆ Arrive in a horse-drawn carriage, every girl's romantic dream.

◆ Cycle in style: you look sweet, upon the seat of a bicycle made for two …

FRANCIS, 25

❝ Our friends travelled from all over the country to come to our wedding, so we nominated a selection of good hotels near the venue and then laid on a bus to do pick-ups and drop-offs to the reception. This way no one got lost or had to worry about drinking. We got our ushers and bridesmaids to go on the buses with them, to introduce everyone and get them all excited. People really appreciated the effort we'd gone to and it didn't cost a fortune. ❞

The great getaway

When your party draws to an end, you and your guests will need to escape before the warm glow chills out and you're cold, hungover, or worse still, sober! Before the big day, talk to the duty manager of the venue to ensure that taxi firm phone numbers are readily available, and ask for the times of the last trains and buses within the vicinity. Better still, organise coaches or minibuses to escort guests to their nearby resting place or transport link.

As for you, my dear, you deserve something a little more special. If your wedding car is still available, hire it to take you wherever you need to be. You'll be calmer and more able to enjoy it when the party is over.

Alternatively, arrange for a mate to drive your car to the venue, so that it's there for you when you want to leave (if one of you isn't drinking and you really love your car!) Tell friends you're doing this, and by the time you leave, it will be festooned with streamers and old tin cans.

If you're having an early, summer wedding – make a real impact by leaving at dusk in a helicopter (most five-star hotels have a helipad, you just need to ask), a bicycle made for two (twee-tastic!) or in a hot air balloon. Even if you land in a field five miles away, the impact will be outrageous – make sure your photographer goes up in the air with you to get some great snaps of you and your Prince Charming.

First night ... so get it right

Where should you spend your first night of wedded bliss? However excited you want to be, the truth is you'll be exhausted, so most couples end up staying overnight at the venue or at a motel near the airport, ready for an early flight the next day.

♦ If you want to do something a bit different – and make an easy escape – go home! Just don't tell anyone. On the morning of the wedding, get a trusted friend to leave a bottle of champers nestling in the fridge next to some smoked salmon, caviar and Belgian chocolates. Pull the curtains, pour yourself some fizz and talk to your new husband – chances are you won't have spent much time together all day. Turn your phones off and have a lie-in.

◆ If you can be bothered, it might be nice to move on to an even posher boutique hotel for the night, away from the wedding-madding crowd. Let them know it's your wedding day, and they should leave fruit and wine in your room for your arrival. Order breakfast in bed, and don't arrange to meet up with anyone until midday at the earliest.

◆ If you can't escape and you're staying in the same place as all your guests, make the most of it. Make sure the bar is kept open so that residents can enjoy a nightcap, then arrange for a trestle table to be set up for breakfast so that you can all sit together and carry on the party.

◆ Some couples want the honeymoon to start as soon as possible, and take a flight out of the country on the evening of the wedding. Make this memorable by upgrading if possible – airlines have offers and differently priced seating. Even reserving leg-room seats and telling them it's your wedding night should make a difference. Be polite, dress smartly, and sweetly enquire about an upgrade. Once on board, have a bottle of champagne and recap your day's highlights.

Secrets of Success

◆ Never say never. The laws on where you can or cannot get married change every year. If you've fallen in love with somewhere, approach your local authorities. Likewise, if your dream is to get married at a particular venue, find out if you can get a special licence.

◆ If your venue is nearly perfect – but something is niggling away at you, go with your instincts and cancel it, or sort it!

Don't lose sleep over something that no one else will even notice.

- If you're getting married in a city, hire a fleet of the flagship taxis to transport the guests, and issue official guides for those who have travelled far.

- Think about getting married in the same church that your parents did. Family tradition means a lot, especially at weddings. My husband and I got married in a church where all of my father's family had tied the knot, and, more poignantly, where my grandparents and great-grandparents are buried.

- If guests are expected to walk from the service to the reception, guide their way with candles, posters, or ribbons in the wedding colours tied around the trees en route.

- How about throwing a party around a pool? Ask guests to bring their swimming gear and lay on lilos and animal inflatables. Make sure you can hire lifeguards – and get them to wear themed T-shirts, or Baywatch-style uniforms. Set up hammocks and cabanas for relaxation and food.

- If your dream location is too expensive, adapt: ask if you can hire just half of the venue; find out if it is cheaper on a weekday or in a different season; or if you can hire the honeymoon suite. You can escape there after your reception and really enjoy it. Another key to saving money on a location is not to say it's your wedding that you wish to hold there – say it's a family gathering. Locations can add on un-needed extra charges when they hear the word 'wedding'!

- Always check who does the clearing up, that you're not expected to and that the venue has insurance for any unforeseen damages, before you sign on the dotted line.

- ◆ Check out the acoustics. If the room is too big and echoey, your guests won't be able to hear the speeches, or worse still, hear each other as they make small talk over dinner.

- ◆ If you have a friend or family member who could officiate at your wedding, it would be a shame not to make the most of this connection – it would ensure you a personalised, sensitive service, so travel to where they are.

- ◆ If your ceremony or party is being held near the river, hire rowing boats for a relaxed journey from the main train station or hotel for guests. Speed boats will get you there a little quicker, and paddle boat steamers – yes, they still exist – will be even cooler.

- ◆ Fleets of minis look stunning – tie in the fabric designs of the men's waistcoats to the go-faster stripes. It sounds mad, but I've known a farmer to arrive to his own wedding on a tractor, and a gardener to arrive astride a ride-on lawnmower. If you're getting married on private farmland or gardens, why not? Make you man's day by arriving in a Ford Gran Torino (à la *Starsky and Hutch*) or a General Lee (from the *Dukes of Hazzard*).

Chapter Three

Seasonal selection

AUTUMN, WINTER, SUMMER, spring ... each season offers
new hope, changing scenery and a different feel. One
of the first big decisions you need to make is which
season is the right time for you to get married.

What things should you consider when you first choose
your wedding date?

1. Are there any special dates you'd like to add your celebration to? Your birthday, your parents' wedding anniversary,
   five years on from the first date you had with your groom?

2. What makes you happy? Sunshine, bracing autumnal
   walks, Christmas? Analyse yourself and your groom.

3. Another, less romantic, reason to choose a certain time is how long will it take you to save up?

4. Will your dream venue be free when you want to get married?

5. External factors may play a part: when is your best friend getting married? When is your baby due and how long will it take you to get your figure back? How long will it take your father to recover from his operation?

Other things aside, when girls imagine their wedding day, they usually picture it as a certain scene – and this scene heavily depends on what time of year you choose to tie the knot. Did you dream of serving mulled wine and wearing a faux-fur cape? Or did you fantasise about holding an Easter egg hunt on the last day of your long weekend of celebrations? Follow your heart. If you've always wanted to be a summer bride, don't allow yourself to be persuaded otherwise by niggling worries or difficulties. You'll regret it.

In this chapter, the positives and negatives of each season will be discussed to help you decide what kind of wedding – and weather – you want. We'll talk about special touches that you can *only* do in this season, the most beautiful colours with which to decorate the rooms and transport, and the best flowers for your bouquet and decoration, as well as the perfect food (although food is discussed more thoroughly in Chapter Five). Let's spring into action.

Spring fever

Spring is fresh and fragrant, green and grassy, lemon-scented and light. Key things that make people think of spring are:

◆ Easter, chocolate and families.

◆ Shrove Tuesday and pancakes.

◆ Bank holidays.

◆ Bulbs and seeds.

◆ Health and fitness, particularly running the marathon.

◆ St Patrick's Day parade.

◆ Rabbits, lambs and chicks.

◆ Fresh air.

◆ Blossom and blooms.

◆ Longer days and warmer weather.

Your spring wedding

This season is all about hope and potential, which is a great beginning to any marriage. The world is exploding with colour and life, and so is your relationship. The key to a spring wedding is to combine the formality of a marriage with the unstoppable power of nature. If you can't hold the wedding outside, make sure you bring the outside inside with fresh colours, gentle fragrance and bursting blooms.

The best colours for this time of year are:

Apple green

Buttercup yellow

Cowslip yellow

Crocus mauve

Duck egg blue

Heath green

Lavender

Lemon yellow

Lichen green

Lilac

Lime green

Olive green

Rose pink

Sage green

SPRING FLOWERS

The world springs to life and it is fresh, green and plentiful again. Breathe in deeply and admire the view – everything is new and full of hope. Lily-of-the-valley makes a delicate, fragrant bouquet at this time of year. It has a touch of elegance combined with innocence, and the flower is shaped like tiny church bells. Peonies are unusual and stunning, and in season in spring. Also, think about:

Allium	*Lathyrus odoratus* (sweet pea)
Daffodil	Orchid
Freesia	Stephanotis
Hyacinth	Tulips

Seasonal special effects

So far, the colours and flowers I have discussed are stunning and classy, and they are the shades and styles that will make the most impact in your chosen season – you're a bride with terribly good taste! Here are some things you could do to turn your spring wedding into a one-off, memorable event:

♦ Print the invitations on handmade paper with pressed flowers.

♦ Give someone else hope and a brighter future: instead of getting three toasters, ask your guests to make a donation to a charity close to your heart.

♦ Make the most of the gentle spring breeze by dangling Tibetan bells and white beads from surrounding trees. They will gently chime and ring as you say your vows.

♦ Instead of a formal bouquet, loosely gather your blooms together with strips of wicker or white satin ribbon.

♦ A friend wanted a non-conformist, spring wedding and was pleased when a nearby farm obtained a wedding licence so that she could hold her wedding in the fragrant orchard. Bright pink apple blossom fell from the swaying trees like confetti, and narcissi lined her makeshift aisle. Magical.

♦ With a bonanza of flowers in season, prices come down, so you can afford to go mad and decorate everywhere. Decorate the end of each pew and windowsill with flowers for the ceremony; attach pots of plants to trees where you exit the service. You could even organise hanging baskets outside the church or civil wedding facility.

♦ Make the flowers even cheaper by buying them directly from markets.

♦ Use bright flowers to guide guests towards the table plan, the guest book or the entrance.

◆ While flowers are reasonably priced, make the most of them and decorate the ladies' toilets too – women spend a lot of time in there gossiping.

◆ If you're tying fresh flowers to the backs of chairs for the service or reception, attach water tubes to those that could wilt. Leave putting them out until the last minute, as there are freakishly hot days in spring.

◆ A nice spring touch is to tie bright yellow ribbon around the trees in the grounds where you are getting hitched.

◆ Wear fresh flowers in your hair, and sod the icing on the cake – cover it with fresh blooms. This is rarely done anymore and looks incredible.

◆ A sprig of fresh blossom tied to each napkin is also a lovely added detail.

◆ Decorate tables with wicker baskets or silver buckets filled with apples, lemons and limes. Write your guests' names on mini-flags and insert them into individual fruits to use as matching place markers.

◆ Gingham is the fabric most associated with spring. Use a pink, blue or yellow gingham for tablecloths, napkin ribbons and invitation ties.

◆ Instead of a formal centrepiece, hang a basket full of weeping, draped plants and flowers from the ceiling above each table.

◆ As wedding favours, you could leave bulbs in brightly coloured pots, or a packet of seeds (perhaps the same as your wedding flowers), on each place setting. They are inexpensive and make everyone look to the future.

◆ Decorate potted-plant centrepieces by covering the soil with crushed tissue paper in your wedding colour then tying a bow around the pot in the same fabric as your bridesmaids' dresses.

◆ Favour boxes in Easter shades of yellow, blue, green and lilac look sweet decorated with mini-fluffy chicks, and are eyecatching piled on side tables. Fill them with luxury handmade chocolates, truffles, mini-eggs, or chocolate, animal-shaped biscuits.

◆ Fill clean jam jars with coloured water and pebbles as an alternative centrepiece.

◆ Toffee and chocolate apples are a great after-dinner treat.

◆ Hire a children's entertainer to dress up as the Easter bunny and instigate a chocolate egg hunt if you have lots of young kids at your bash.

◆ Make edible bird's nests from breakfast cereal and chocolate and fill them with sweets.

◆ Ask an artist to draw or paint the flower or plant you had on your table, and print the work as a thank-you card.

SPRING DRESSING

Early spring allows you to carry through the elements of winter that you like, such as long sleeves or a cape. For more of a spring feel, however, go for flowery embroidery and a butterfly or bee detail on the veil. Wear fresh flowers in your hair or a flower-inspired tiara. Whereas white is easy to get away with on a bright day if your face has a healthy glow, spring pastels can be even more flattering for dresses. More about this in the next chapter. Keep make-up light and pretty – lots of highlighter on the cheeks and lip gloss.

Spring food and drink

This is the best time of the year to serve light, fruity cocktails, cordials and cider to drink. Meals shouldn't be too heavy, but the emphasis should be on fresh, colourful vegetables in season, flavoured with fresh herbs and butter.

Desserts should be light and fruity – fresh berries and cream, for example, is naughty but nice. A different, unique meal idea is to serve a sumptuous farmhouse style of tea: trestle tables stacked high with scones, jams, fairy cakes and meats highlights the abundance of springtime. My friend – a farmer's daughter – was married on their own farmland, and served a traditional Cornish tea, while lambs and rabbits hopped around us. It was a magical day, and not too hot! This would be harder to do at the peak of summer.

Spring nightmares

- ◆ Beware of insects. Burn citronella candles in the evening, if outside.

- ◆ April showers. Say no more.

- ◆ Hay fever, the curse of many at this time of year.

- ◆ Kids will be revising for their exams.

- ◆ Football fixtures and finals.

> **LISA, 30**
>
> ❝ I'm a complete chocoholic, and when our dream wedding venue – an old castle – had a free date on Good Friday, we thought it was fate. We had to get married there and we had to have a chocolate wedding. A chocolatier near our home made chocolate horseshoes for good luck, which we left on the tables. We had a chocolate fountain, a six foot white chocolate wedding cake (yes, it can be done!) ... and hot chocolate at midnight to bid the guests farewell. Where did we go on our honeymoon? We could only take a long weekend because of business commitments so – believe it or not – we went to Belgium for even more chocolate. Heaven! ❞

Summer lovin'

If you would love to have a warm and wonderful big day, the summer is the season for you. Everyone is in a good mood – they've either just been on holiday or have got one to look forward to. Hot and hazy, light and breezy, what does summer make people think of?

- Sunshine and sun-kissed skin.

- Summer solstice.

- Midsummer eve.

- Cocktails and parties.

- Bright lights and long days.

- Bikinis and barbecues.

- Holidays and happiness.

♦ Staying up all night, sunsets and sunrises.

♦ Vibrant colours.

♦ Ice cream!

Your summer wedding

June is the most popular month to get married in Britain, and it's easy to see why. The three months of summer have the latest sunsets, the least rain, the bluest skies ... what's not to like? Your wedding should celebrate the vibrancy of living, the joy of the outside, the happiness people feel around this time of year. Colours to reflect a long, hot summer include:

Bronze

Buttercup yellow

Fuchsia

Gold

Paprika red

Raspberry pink

Scarlet

White

SUMMER FLOWERS

You've picked the best month for colourful blooms. Celebrate with bright, bountiful displays of all colours. When she married in the garden of her New York home, the effortlessly stylish actress Julianne Moore got her florist to make stunning cast-iron urns of clematis, honeysuckle and the sweetly named love-in-a-puff! Yum, you can imagine the smell! Also think about:

Centaurea cyanus (cornflower)
Consolida (larkspur)
Dahlia
Delphinium
Lavender
Lily
Magnolia
Matthiola (stock)
Peony
Polianthes tuberosa (tuberose)

Seasonal special effects

◆ If you're having a beach wedding, why not go the whole way and become the Little Mermaid. Instead of wearing a tiara, try a summer-blossom headdress, and carry a handful of palm leaves and hibiscus flowers. Put the groomsmen in Hawaiian shirts and leis and give the flower girls baskets of seashells to hand out to guests. Leaving the party? Would a surfboard be too silly?

◆ And if you really love the sea, you can take it even further and get married underwater. OK, you may look like a drowned rat in your scuba gear but it will be unique! Perhaps hold a blessing on shore afterwards – your Great Aunt Mabel may not be good with sharks!

◆ Attach tiny seashells to your bouquet with lace from your veil or dress.

◆ And then of course, you can get married naked. Oh yes, in Hawaii there is even a vicar who will perform the ceremony starkers for you. This is a good way to cut the guest list.

◆ If you're on a tight budget, why not take to the high seas – or at least a river or lake – for the reception? The glimmering water will add instant sparkle on a sunny day, and cut the costs of hiring an expensive venue. For example, to hire a venue overlooking the Thames would cost a fortune but you can hire a disco boat to cruise up and down it for a few hundred pounds.

◆ On a very hot day, provide white fans or Chinese parasols for the ladies. They look elegant and are a timeless keepsake.

◆ Why not have a pool party to end all pool parties. Many registered venues have outdoor swimming areas or spas, where guests can chill out while supping champers in the sun. Make a note on the invitations to tell everyone to bring a swimming costume.

◆ Hand out colour-themed parasols to female guests, if the service is outside. These can be pricey so, if need be, hire or borrow them. They don't need to match – they can be boho-chic.

◆ For an unusual table piece, think about installing aquariums or mini-fishbowls, or forget the fish and have ornate bowls of water with floating candles and petals.

◆ A Raj-style tent in bedazzling jewel colours will make a perfect outdoor area in which to serve food and drink.

◆ Large, church candles can look too much at a summer wedding – instead opt for coloured fairy lights.

◆ Choose a menu of barbecued and grilled foods and decorate the platters with edible petals.

◆ Keep your booze cool by installing a mini-refrigerator on each table. They come with different designs and colours; opt for one that suits your theme or personality.

◆ Take guests back to their childhood: leave sticks of rock on each place setting, and have them personalised with the name of your town or the date of your wedding running through the middle.

◆ Theme your wedding around the seaside – fly bunting between the trees, serve fish and chips, cockles and mussels, and old-fashioned lemonade. Use blue-and-white stripy tablecloths and throw shells and pebbles on all the surfaces. Make paper boats to use as place markers. Perhaps make a mini-beach – with sand, windbreakers and beach balls – as a posing area for the pictures.

◆ Leave cheap and cheerful flip-flops for the women as a wedding favour. Pretty, sequined and one-size-fits-all – you can pick them up quite cheaply, and what a useful present!

◆ Hire a steel-drum band – nothing says summer quicker, even if you are stuck in a grey city centre.

◆ If it's a really hot day, pop to your local DIY or toy store and buy a selection of water sprays, paddling pools and water pistols to put in the gardens. Act with decorum until the pictures are completed – then go for soak!

◆ Tie the music into the mood – hot weather welcomes samba or salsa.

◆ Lure people outside by burning outdoor heaters. If there's a point of interest (a lake, statues, and so on) that you want to be enjoyed, put the heaters there and your guests will follow them.

SUMMER DRESSING

Keep cool in floaty, light fabrics and loose-fitting silk. Forget the stockings and suspenders – they'll itch in the heat. Empire-line and shift dresses suit this season, and you can forget the added extras like shrugs and bolero jackets. Make sure your hair and make-up won't wilt in the heat; ask your mother or bridesmaid to keep some spare mascara and lip gloss in case yours slides down your face. Anti-shine powder is also a good idea.

Summer food and drink

Avoid things that will look sweaty or greasy – or give you food poisoning – if left in the heat. This is the time of year to eat fish with fresh lemon, mint and new potatoes, which go perfectly with white wine, champagne and rosé. Avoid anything too rich or heavy. Strawberries dipped in white chocolate are amazing served with ice-cold Pimms and lemonade. Lollipops tied with ribbon make good wedding favours.

Summer nightmares

◆ The heat (make sure there's plenty of shade, and water for guests to drink).

◆ Insects and animals – watch out for lurking creepy crawlies.

◆ People tend to book their holidays at this time of year.

◆ Most people hold their weddings now, so your guests may be double-booked.

◆ Squinting in photos.

SUE, BEAUTY THERAPIST

❝ I got married in Santa Barbara, California, so I learnt a lot of tips about keeping hair and make-up looking good in the heat. Firstly, I'd buy a leave-in conditioner, which you can spray in before you go to the beach. It has a barrier in it to stop your hair drying out in the sun. In the weeks before the wedding, leave conditioner on for 20 minutes, and then rinse with cold water – it shuts the hair follicle down to make your hair look shinier. Stop make-up sliding off your face by putting a refining or cooling mask on your face before putting on your make-up; cucumber or mint masks are good. It closes your pores, refines your skin and calms everything down. Because of this you won't secrete any oils, which make you look shiny. It's a perfect base for make-up, helping it to stay on for longer. After you've done your make-up, add a light dusting of translucent powder to keep everything in place. ❞

Ode to autumn

'Season of mists and mellow fruitfulness', said the great English poet, Keats. It was his favourite season, and my husband's too – hence our October wedding. Autumn reminds us of:

◆ Bonfires and Guy Fawkes.

◆ Fireworks and sparklers.

◆ Rustling leaves and crunchy pavements.

◆ Fog and wind and dark nights indoors.

◆ Log fires and brandy.

◆ Conkers and acorns.

◆ Hallowe'en.

◆ Apple-bobbing and candyfloss.

Your autumn wedding

Autumn is the time when everything changes again, but instead of the year's decline feeling sad, it's comfy and reassuring. Colours should reflect the tones of nature as it prepares for the cold months, and the warmth of the family home:

Aubergine	Pewter grey
Bronze	Plum
Emerald green	Russet red
Orange	

AUTUMN FLOWERS

This is the changing season, where leaves fall and deepen in colour, and the evenings draw in and the temperature drops. Conkers are used as a championship sport, and colour is hard to find. Think about:

Amaryllis	Hosta
Aster	Hydrangea
Chrysanthemum	Hypericum
Clematis	

Seasonal special effects

◆ Make the most of both worlds – autumn is hot and cold. Do your photos outside, then rush in to a warm, candlelit room for the reception. Decorate the room with tea lights; they are inexpensive, last for about four hours and are small enough to be put everywhere without being overpowering.

◆ This is the season where foliage comes into its own – wonderful colours and large displays can be created cheaply from twigs and leaves. Use your imagination.

◆ Cut-out pumpkins make fabulous – and reasonable – autumn table decorations; just don't make the faces too scary or you'll upset small children. Also put them at entrances, in the loos and on the bar.

◆ Shine up some conkers, tie on to mini-name tags, and leave them as markers for people's places.

◆ Dry leaves and scatter them across the table for a seasonal touch.

◆ If you're getting hitched around Bonfire Night, put mini-sparklers in the desserts, and hand out normal ones to all guests for when they bid you farewell at the end of the night.

◆ ... and you really should have a firework display as well! Even if it's just your brothers running around with a few rockets (carefully of course!) If you are doing this, make sure the best man, or master of ceremonies, announces it clearly so that everyone can gather outside. Perhaps have the display to mark the start of the evening disco, or the end of the evening. If you can arrange for the bangs and explosions to be set to music, even better. Don't go so far as to have Guy dummies made of you and your groom for burning, though – that is bad taste.

◆ Set up a fun room with apple-bobbing and a candyfloss machine.

◆ Cheap-and-cheerful food is easy at this time of year: everyone loves a baked potato with butter. Serve with big containers of baked beans, coleslaw and cheese. If this seems too plain, spice it up with chillies, nachos and sour cream.

◆ Bangers and mash, with onion gravy, goes down a treat with fireworks.

◆ Hallowe'en is growing in popularity beyond the US now, so go for a kitsch wedding reception: cover ceilings and corners with black and orange netting, fill with balloons. Sprinkle special metallic confetti over surfaces – you can get mini-pumpkins, witches, skeletons. If you really want to go for it, persuade the waiting staff to wear fluorescent skull-and-bones costumes when they serve the drinks.

◆ Leave tricks and treats on each table to entertain the guests between courses. For example, they can keep their lottery ticket if they tell everyone around the table something they've never told anyone before. This will cause much amusement.

◆ A Bloody Mary makes the perfect Hallowe'en drink – chuck in an edible or plastic eyeball for effect.

◆ Get a mixologist in to set up a spooky-monster bar: lots of green and orange slime served in sugared glasses, and decorated with physalis. If he can get steam coming out of the glass, even better!

◆ Hey, its harvest-festival time – what about giving guests a luxury hamper as a wedding favour. If you can't run to that, just a pot of jam or marmalade (gooseberry, blackberry or champagne-infused) will be great. Make your own personalised labels, and tie with ribbon to match your bouquet or the bridesmaids' dresses.

AUTUMN DRESSING

The temptation to go for gold is at its maximum in this season – but it can be too heavy for pale skins. The most flattering shade for all is ivory, so just add some intricate gold stitching to the train and veil if you want to introduce it on your outfit. However, be careful about going too heavy with brocade and rich fabrics, such as fake fur and velvet – September and October can be very warm! Err on the side of caution and have a wrap or jacket that can be taken off when things heat up.

Autumn food

Warm guests up with intense flavours – orange, cinnamon and ginger are all wonderful seasonal seasonings, and they smell incredible, of course. Support the menu by burning fragranced candles as guests enter for pre-dinner drinks. Guests will appreciate a warm meal: start with a toasted mushroom or Stilton tart, then move on to a heavy, fulfilling meat course, with a suitable vegetarian alternative. Caramel, toffee and chocolate are great to round off the meal. Fill your guests' glasses with hearty red wines and dry whites. A whisky cocktail is an added bonus.

Autumn nightmares

◆ Rain, drizzle and dreary days make mud an inevitability.

◆ Strong winds can cause problems for your veil.

◆ Blue skies? Forget it. It's grey all the way, normally.

◆ As the cold sets in, you may have coughing through your vows.

◆ Flowers, fruit and vegetables get less varied and more expensive.

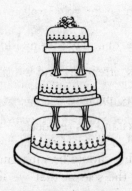

BECKY, 25

❛ Everyone thought we were mad getting married in November but in a way it freed us up from the usual worries of brides – the weather! Yes it rained, yes it was grey and windy but it made it all the more atmospheric. We filled the church with orange and lime ribbons, and balanced clusters of orange tulips on each pew. By 5.00 p.m. it was dark, and we gathered in a candlelit room, drinking punch and munching on chipolata and onion mash canapés. As a wedding favour we gave out hot water bottles in orange faux-fur to the women and hip flasks to the men. ❜

Winter wonderland

Ice, ice baby... snow, snow, snow... jingle bells, jingle bells – the songs say it all! Christmas is the perfect time for tying the knot if you want a cosy, family day. Winter makes us think of:

◆ Parties and pantomimes.

◆ Snowflakes and icicles.

◆ Classic films and cheesy pop music.

◆ Wrapping up warm and gathering indoors.

◆ Silly games, hats, streamers and whistles.

◆ Presents, presents, presents!

◆ Father Christmas and his reindeers.

Your winter wedding should be snug and reassuring, full of the best things of the season that we look forward to all year round. It's the time when everyone gets close and gossips, and drinks and eats too much. The décor should reflect this. The perfect colours for the room and your bouquet are:

Berry red	Indigo
Bronze	Purple
Charcoal grey	Rich green
Dove grey	Silver
Gold	White

WINTER FLOWERS

This is the time of year to go deep and warm: a clutched bouquet of deep red ranunculus and cockscomb, tied together with velvet ribbon is perfectly exuberant. Or you could go icy and cool: spray dried flowers and leaves with silver paint or snowflake powder. Flowers will be expensive at this time of the year, so fill out your displays with twigs, berries and foliage. Grand displays work well, especially around Christmas and New Year. As the eye is used to seeing elaborate decorations add more for a wedding. Think about:

Galanthus (snowdrop)	Mistletoe
Gaultheria (snowberries)	Phlox
Holly	Pine
Hyacinth	Rose
Iris	Tulip
Ivy	

Winter special effects

◆ Save money by sending out Christmas cards as invitations.

◆ Think about arriving on a horse-drawn sleigh.

◆ Walk to the party carrying lanterns.

◆ Make a stunning entrance with dry ice and smoke – provided by the DJ.

◆ Pass round cups of steaming cider with cinnamon or mulled wine as guests arrive, it will keep their fingers from turning blue while they wait for the bride.

◆ Cover the ceremony venue with ivory, red or green candles in hurricane sleeves and votives.

◆ Pin red crystals and tiny pearls to napkins and flower arrangements.

◆ The most traditional colour scheme is to use green, red and gold in a Christmas scene, but it's unusual to hold weddings at this time of the year, so what a great excuse to be unique and old-fashioned at the same time.

◆ Check with the venue what their Christmas decorations are like and when they are going up. If they're fabulous – hoorah, you've saved some money. If not, make sure you've got time to get them down, and a good friend to put them back up the next day.

◆ This is the season to sparkle: fairy lights, glitter, candles – don't hold back!

◆ Keep everything ice cool with crisp, plain linen and china, and polished silver cutlery. And use sprayed silver twigs and leaves as a table centrepiece.

◆ Decorate windows with a snowflake design – ask the venue first, though.

◆ Drape ivy and clusters of berries from each surface.

◆ Be mischievous: tie mistletoe above doors and exits.

◆ Hang decorative stockings from fireplaces, and add interest to dull areas by adding tinsel and baubles. A fir tree in the entrance will give real wow power, and add a beautiful smell to the room.

◆ Leave plain or spray-painted fir cones as place markers, or candy cones with brown labels attached on each seat.

◆ Crackers need to be pulled at this time of the year, so leave them on each setting.

◆ Get a children's entertainer – or your granddad – to dress up as Father Christmas, and sing carols while he hands out gifts to the under-14s.

◆ To warm up a grey, dull day think about having an Arabian Nights theme. The decadent, dark fabrics and candlelight will encourage guests to snuggle up and chill out on large cushions under canopied ceilings.

◆ Leave beautifully wrapped gifts for all the men and women in big sacks at the exit, with a thank-you note attached.

◆ Hey, don't forget this is the time of year to welcome in the New Year. If you're having a New Year's Eve or New Year's Day wedding, go mad on all good party basics – we need lots of streamers, blowers, party poppers, tambourines, trumpets, and so on. Make midnight special – chime in the sounds of Big Ben, have the DJ ready with 'Auld Lang Syne', kick your legs to 'New York, New York' in a circle. This is New Year *and* your wedding –

this party has got to rock into the early hours of the morning. Make sure the bar won't stop serving at 11.00 p.m.

◆ Taxis will be a nightmare, so think about laying on buses or coaches. Carry on the theme by decorating them with ribbon, and make sure there is a music system on board. Also, make sure guests book their accommodation early or there'll be no room at the inn.

◆ Don't forget the other big celebration of winter: St Valentine's Day on 14 February. Pull everyone out of their winter slump with romance, romance, romance. Hey, wear a red dress, if it suits you. Dress the pageboys as cupids. Serve heart-shaped fruit mousse for dessert. Print up love notes and leave them in places for people to find – and give to guests they've been admiring. Lots of people fall in love at other people's weddings – use yours as an excuse to do some matchmaking!

WINTER DRESSING

Everything rich and luxurious works at this time of the year – be as decadent as you ever dreamed. Turn into an ice princess with lashings of diamonds and jewels. Use feathers, use ribbon, use lace. Use faux fur to cover up during the ceremony before unveiling a slinky, red dress for the party. If you want traditional elegance, a long-sleeved duchess satin dress is timeless – make it unique by sewing your wedding date or names in intricate pearls on the train.

Winter food

Mulled wine, dry sherry and eggnog are winter winners. Keep things souper-douper by serving a rich broth as a starter, with delicious breads and butter. Everyone feels hungriest in cold weather, so don't scrimp on the main course. In fact, what about serving a Christmas dinner with all the trimmings? Finish off with something comforting and familiar – no poncey profiteroles or mousses. Treacle tart, apple crumble or sticky toffee pudding with cream and custard will make your guests feel loved. Finish off with an extra – or serve as a later buffet – of cheeses, fruits and chutneys, washed down with a celebratory glass of port.

Winter problems

- ◆ Hangovers. Guests may have overdone it during the party season and feel less than great.

- ◆ Family commitments might mean a lot of 'Sorry we can't accept' replies.

- ◆ Flights and long-distance travel is most expensive at this time of year. Freak weather can make roads impassable.

- ◆ Colds and flu can set in and send a quarter of the guests to bed early.

JEN, 31

❝ My new husband's called Noel, so we couldn't not have a Christmas wedding, could we? We held it a few days after Christmas, which worked out well, as those in-between days are when everyone finishes off the cold turkey and sits around watching crap telly until New Year's Eve. Our friends and family loved extending the festive week – and putting on their glad rags. There was not a slice of turkey in sight – we thought our guests would be up for something a bit more exotic after lots of home cooking, so we treated them to a Hungarian goulash with chunks of bread and red wine, followed by ice cream. It was cold, but different from the heavy, rich cakes everyone had been living on for days. ❞

Secrets of Success

◆ The great thing about weddings is the freedom using the great outdoors can bring. I've been to weddings where the couple have hired bouncy castles, trampolines and those Velcro-elastic running machines. They bring instant adrenalin to any event.

◆ Try to see the venue in the season you will be getting married in. Full trees may cover a power plant at the back of your church in spring, but in autumn? Check the view!

◆ Make sure your venue can cope with emergencies, such as snowstorms and heatwaves.

◆ Choose a seasonal theme that's close to your heart; if it's a last-minute whim, it's likely to show.

- ◆ Get to know the local area – do they hold summer carnivals or winter festivals on your chosen wedding day that might affect your celebration?

- ◆ Ask if there will be any major roadworks near your venue at the time of your wedding.

- ◆ Madonna stops her lips drying out in summer or winter by adding a little Carex lip balm to her lipsticks and glosses before applying. This will also keep the colour on for longer on hot days. Get the season's best celebrity beauty tips from your favourite magazines.

Chapter Four

Dress to impress

THIS IS YOUR DAY, AND I DON'T want to freak you out, but everyone will be staring at you. Every woman will want to know where you got your dress, how high your heels are, if your tiara is handmade, and so on. Women love fairy tales and they love a fairy princess. Don't disappoint. Don't do a Pamela Anderson and exchange your vows in a white bikini – unless it's always been your aim!

The bride

How to choose your dress?

What every girl should remember when picking her dress:

1. Confidence does wonders for anyone. Make sure you love the dress and you know you look beautiful.

2. The size on the label is irrelevant; it's how it fits your unique shape that matters.

3. Don't be smutty. Be sexy. No one likes a vicar with an erection. Choose a low-cut back or a side-split in the skirt rather than full on boobs-out-there cleavage and miniskirt combo. Unless you really want to, of course.

4. If you're short and you want to stand out – wear heels. If you're tall and don't want to tower over your groom – wear flats. What works for you will work for your wedding.

5. Don't be scared to look feminine and seductive. So what if you normally wear jeans and jumpers.

6. No one has a perfect body – the dress designer or shop assistant has seen it all before and isn't judging you ...

7. ... but all women have a good point, or a few if they're lucky. Find yours and celebrate it. Women tend to feel self-conscious of tummies and bottoms, but wedding dresses give you the chance to show off the perfect regions, that is, the shoulders, or the back, or the décolletage.

8. If you want to look slim, or get an hourglass effect, keep everything flat in the stomach area, and use ruching, draping and tucking at the chest and bottom.

9. Fabric is important. The best for a smooth silhouette are silk, satin and viscose, which aren't bulky. Add hoops and petticoats for volume (you can remove these in the evening when you want to dance.) If you want a train for the service, ask the dressmaker to make a tiny stitch or button for you at the back, which will enable you to hook it up neatly. I did this and it was a lifesaver – I wouldn't have been able to get on the floor to do 'Oops Upside Your Head' without it!

10. Only go shopping with people you can trust. And make sure that wherever you go has a big, comfortable changing room with massive mirrors and that the assistants give you their exclusive attention. No bride-to-be wants this decision to be hurried. Try on as many designs as you can bear – even ones that don't take your fancy on the hanger.

Celebrity style

What can we learn from the famous princess brides? Well, Victoria Beckham did the obvious celebrity thing and went to New York to get a design by Vera Wang. Luckily, Wang's style is now so famous in its own right that you can pick up a similar dress, hinting at her elegant style, much cheaper. Sarah Michelle Gellar also went for Vera's classic bodice style when she married fellow Hollywood star, Freddie Prinze Jr.

Carmen Electra chose the other celeb bridal designer, Badgley Mischka, when she married her rocker lover, Dave Navarro. She paired her classic dress with sexy white fishnet tights!

The queen of the A-list, Catherine Zeta-Jones, asked the catwalk's most dazzling star, Christian Lacroix, to design her wedding dress – and Michael couldn't have looked happier with the result. The fitted V-neck gown – with a super-long train – sparkled and hugged her curves amazingly. Stunning!

Jennifer Aniston asked a designer who had worked with her on Oscar outfits to make her dress: Lawrence Steele. The floor-length, bias-cut dress was backless (very sexy) and covered in tiny pearls. Brad Pitt couldn't have been more appreciative.

Joan Collins played the classic mature bride in a flattering lavender number, with a dramatic neckline and sleeves, and a simple matching flower decoration in her hair.

Celeb brides are all very much into veils – even modern diva Jennifer Lopez wore one at her recent wedding to Latino crooner Marc Anthony. She also carried a parasol – but that might be too much for your unstarry wedding, who knows?

NB I would say the wedding dress is the one area where you should show caution and not go hell-for-leather in your bid to be unique, like many of the stars have done. And you don't want to regret your choice. Also, believe me, photos of you in the ill-chosen monstrosity can haunt you forever. However much you love something, if your mother, best friend and the shop manager are grinning nervously – learn from it. If you've really got your heart set on a hillbilly ensemble with suede cowboy boots, save it for the evening or, even better, as your going-away outfit.

Bride's-dress revisited

This may be a ghastly idea, but what was your mum's wedding dress like – and does she still have it? Or even your grandma's or your new mother-in-law's? I've only ever seen one bride wearing a dress with real family significance, and it really made a difference. The families were happy and all the other women spent ages looking at the fabric and the craftsmanship. Ask around, and if you're in luck, go to a good dressmakers to discuss with them about getting it cleaned, fitted and updated. If it's truly hideous, ask if you can just cut a small piece from the petticoat – and pin it to your own for good luck.

Colour chameleon

The truth is, the traditional white wedding dress is rarely white – it's normally ivory or oyster pink. White can be very harsh, but if you have a tan it can look stunning – and look very crisp and fresh compared to the usual off-white varieties we see today.

But do you have to stick to these light shades? Well, there is something magical about a bride in the 'virginal' shade, but there can be something breathtaking about other colours, too.

When I went wedding-dress shopping with my mother a year before my wedding, my eyes fell upon a lavender number which my mother said I should try on – just to convince myself it was wrong. Well, it wasn't – this big lilac meringue was stunning! We loved it. But I chickened out of buying it and settled for an ivory gown. Why? I was worried about what people – and my groom – would think when the Sugar Plum Fairy entered the church. Should I have cared? Probably not. I still think back to that dress and how the colour suited me more than the ivory. So remember, girls: if something suits you and you love it, don't regret things later – just buy it.

Saying this, I have seen a bride in a large purple gown and gawped in horror. Purple was her favourite colour, so everything had to match: she wore a purple dress, purple shoes, purple veil – even purple lipstick. When we sang a line from 'All Things Bright and Beautiful' in the church, 'that purple-headed mountain', the congregation disintegrated into giggles. She was a rather large girl and the colour did nothing to exaggerate the positives and hide the negatives.

So if you do love a colour, and want to wear it at your wedding, perhaps go to a colour analyst first to make sure it suits your hair and skin, and brings out the colour of your eyes. Then don't overdo it. Wear it, but don't dress the whole wedding party in the same shade – and definitely match your make-up to your face, not to your dress.

- ◆ If you have red hair/pale skin try pale green, burnt orange or light blue.

- ◆ If you have blonde hair/pale skin try pale blue, light pink or soft yellow.

- ◆ If you have blonde hair/dark skin try bright pink, aquamarine or yellow.

- ◆ If you have brown hair/dark skin try red, pink, yellow, gold or bronze.

- ◆ If you have black hair/dark skin try orange, lime green or purple.

LOUISE, 40

❝ During my first trying-on of dresses session with my sister, I had a clear idea in my head of what I wanted ... but I tried on everything. It's the only way to make sure you don't regret it or feel you've missed out. The other thing is colour: it's so easy to stick to white and cream, but my sister persuaded me to try on a red dress – and I loved it. It suited my skin tone completely and I felt really confident. My husband got a bit of a shock – and of course there were a few raised eyebrows – but I've never worried about those! It matched my ruby engagement ring and made me feel very confident and sexy. ❞

Fabric fantastic

Why stick to silk tulle when the world is full of amazing material? Hip new fabric choices that are being snapped up by dress designers include:

- Mohair (adds instant cuteness).

- Lace (antique and dyed are chic).

- Sari silks (for colour and easy-wearing).

- Netting (for that fab 1950s approach).

- Cashmere (people won't be able to keep their hands off you).

- Cotton (for a laid-back look).

- Chiffon (for instant girlishness).

And, designers are going even more mad for ribbon, beading, sequins, gems, layering, pearls, and so on. I recently saw an incredible dress that looked very plain and simple but the whole underneath was covered with Swarovski crystals. As the bride walked or danced, it caught the light in the most dazzling, subtle way. It was most unusual but classically beautiful.

If you have an idea about what fabric and detail you want, don't settle for anything else. If you find a style you like, most designers will be able to work across different materials – which may cost you more, but you'll get what you want.

Dress for your do

Your dress must not only suit you, but it must also suit your wedding venue. Remember that or you'll stand out for all the wrong reasons.

◆ Small venue: a big dress is overwhelming; go for neat, fitted and figure-hugging.

◆ Grand venue: don't overdo the accessories; you'll be competing with the chandeliers. Make the big gestures with the actual dress – with a long train, for example.

◆ Country venue: avoid high heels, tight skirts and long trains – anything that could be tricky to deal with on muddy grass and paths.

◆ City venue: ditch the meringue; go for formal and sophisticated.

◆ Cocktail reception: again, no meringues, in fact knee-length is best. If you are flashing flesh, make sure skin is tanned, moisturised and hair-free where it should be. Tights or stockings should be flesh-coloured – except if you want to make your legs look longer by matching shoe and stocking colour.

ALL DAY AND ALL NIGHT

Adapt your outfit from the daytime ceremony to evening reception by:

• Removing shrugs, capes and overcoats.

• Taking off excessive hoop skirts or petticoats.

• Pinning up a long train into a handy bustle.

• Adding new, sparkling jewels such as a choker.

• Putting on dancing shoes that are charmingly glitzy.

• Taking down your hair and wearing it loose.

• Applying glitter spray to your décolletage.

• Wearing a darker shade of lipstick.

Suit yourself

Who can forget the amazing picture of Bianca Jagger at her wedding to Mick, looking effortlessly glam in a white Yves Saint Laurent trouser suit? Wow, she turned heads. Tuxedo and heels is a classic, killer look. But it takes guts to wear it. If you want to go down this route, hint around the idea to your groom. Some men would find it a massively cool turn-on, others would be disappointed that the woman of their dreams has chosen to wear something she could wear to work. If he's okay with it, and you're not getting married in a church (the vicar would swallow his bible, and aisles can seem long in killer heels), get shopping.

Don't think that because you're not getting a grand dress you don't have to spend as much money. Oh no. If you want to pull off the suit look, you need to do it well. This means going to a top tailor of a couture house (why not investigate YSL and Chanel on Ebay?) and pay big bucks. Get measured properly, and, like a dress, get it fitted to you and perfected shortly before the big day.

If you find trouser suits too masculine, skirt suits are a good in-between. The jacket can be discarded in the evening to make a different look – wear a sequined or cashmere vest underneath.

You don't have to stick to white, as it can be harsh on certain skins. If you're going for a suit, you might as well go for a suit you feel comfortable enough in to wear again and again. Follow the aforementioned colour rules and ask a good, honest friend what she thinks. Just avoid clashing colours, patterns or fabric; the whole idea of a bridal suit is to look understated and gorgeous, not like a three-piece suite.

AGE-OLD CONCERNS

If you're a mature bride, there are a few easy rules you can follow to look marvellous:

- Don't wear a hat, that's mother-of-the-bride territory.

- Carry a bouquet to reinforce your bridal status.

- Ask a personal shopper for unbiased, constructive advice.

- Look like yourself, just better.

- Avoid white, which can be cruel for older, pale skin.

- Wear one spectacular piece of jewellery to distract eyes from elsewhere.

- Chignons and up-dos can be too harsh, so wear hair loose.

Head girl

The next most important thing after your dress is what you wear on your head. Traditionally, a tiara or crown of flowers is worn, but spice up the look with:

◆ A ring of roses.

◆ A daisy chain.

◆ An Alice band.

◆ A sheer headscarf.

◆ Feathers.

◆ Velvet ribbon.

◆ A square of vintage lace.

◆ A string of pearls.

◆ Mini-diamanté hair clips.

◆ Mother-of-pearl hair slides.

If you're going for a tiara, instead of choosing plain crystal, pick out the colours in your bouquet or the bridesmaids' dresses and tie them in. Choose drop pearls that dangle on to your forehead. Wear a small tiara pinned around a bun. Pin a small tiara to the side, with your hair swept on to the opposite shoulder. Borrow your mother's or grandmother's tiara.

If you're wearing your hair down, spray it with a shine and/or glitter spray for extra pizzazz. Make sure it has been cut well beforehand, and your roots have been sorted out a few days prior to the wedding. A good blow-dry will complete the look.

Veils are slightly out of favour at the moment, but I think they complete the bridal look. Update a bit of dull netting by having it embroidered with your names or the date of your wedding or by having beads, pearls and jewels sewn on to the edge. You don't have to have the full, long veil; the new trend is to have a mini, shoulder-length veil reminiscent of Jackie Onassis and Britt Ekland.

Best foot forward

Most of the time your feet will be covered by your dress, so don't get distressed if you can't afford a pair of Manolo Blahniks. If you can, marvellous! Check when buying super-pricey shoes that they can be dyed to a more useful colour after your big day.

Practise walking in the shoes a few weeks before the wedding; sadly a limping bride isn't a unique sight when the bride's in three-inch heels and hasn't worn them in.

I met a brilliant shoe designer recently and she makes wedding shoes extra special by adding words and pictures to the shoe in tiny crystals. Think about having 'I do' on each toe, or the groom's name. Other brides have chosen to have their country's flag on the heel, or the date of their wedding. It's an extra touch that makes your outfit even more special. Other shoe-in ideas include:

◆ Ballet pumps are great if you are the same height or taller than the groom.

◆ If it's warm and appropriate, go barefoot for hippy-chic.

◆ Flip-flops – decorated with beads and shells – are fab for beach dos.

◆ It's rarely necessary to wear boots at a wedding, but if you love your baby pink Uggs, why not?

◆ Trainers are marvellous – not only are they white but also they make it possible to dance all night long.

AMAZING ACCESSORIES

Other cool touches to think about for a unique wedding look are:

- Fur stoles (fake, please, ladies).
- Flamenco-style fans.
- Cowgirl hats.
- Pashminas.
- Parasols.
- Brooches.
- Satin elbow-length gloves.
- Sequined clutch bags.
- Lace overcoats.

Something ...

Old: look for family antique jewellery to display or pin for good luck, or ask a friend for whom you were a bridesmaid if you could use her veil or tiara.

New: your dress covers this, but something special could be a new fragrance that you've bought to match your bouquet.

Borrowed: treat yourself to some real bling bling, and hire some jaw-dropping diamonds from a jeweller or designer. Who cares if they have to go back the next morning?

Blue: a chameleon brooch is timeless, so are sapphire stud earrings. If you're looking for something cheaper, add one simple bluebell or iris to your bouquet, or stitch a square of blue silk ribbon to your corset.

Underneath your clothes

Why stop all the uniqueness of your outfit at the dress? To please my husband on our wedding night – don't worry, I'm not getting too personal – I decorated my thigh with a West Ham United suspender belt. I'm a Spurs fan so my husband knew this meant a lot. And he loved it. Try the same by wearing your man's football or rugby team colours or badge on your underwear – and if you're lucky, it will incorporate the 'something blue'. Visit the club shop or website.

The other big thing that celebrities are going crazy for at the moment is side-tie, bow knickers. You can get them with wording, sequins, holes (!?) – oh yes, frilly knickers are very much the order of the day.

I once heard of an extremely brave bride who donned her new husband's white cotton boxers under her dress, as a sign of her taking him completely. He found it very sexy apparently!

And now to more erotic underwear that you could be tempted to kick-start your wedding with. Well, edible knickers taste disgusting – and have a tendency to stick to clothing and pubic hair (ouch!), so avoid those. Surveys always state men find red underwear the most exciting, but pink or white is more bridal, so find a lacy, delicate small thing in one of these colours.

Some very understanding wives have been known to wear a mini-nurse or policewoman's uniform under their wedding dress – but seriously, laydeez, you're going to be hot and uncomfortable as it is. Save any original ideas you have for erotic underwear for the honeymoon, you'll have plenty of time there – and won't be making small talk with your grandma while wearing it.

A couple I know avoided the overly sexy thing and wore matching tartan pyjamas to bed, which was just as well, because their room was ram-raided by over-zealous, drunken pals at 3.00 a.m.

> **NB But if a simple white G-string and strapless bra** is the best route for your wedding gown, wear those. Simply pack the bustier/teddy/plastic nurse's uniform into your overnight bag. Seeing fluorescent pink knickers shining through your ivory silk dress would totally ruin the effect.

The party people

The wedding isn't just about the bride (well, we'll pretend that) so to complete your unique, gorgeous wedding the other important members of the group should look memorably stylish too. Here's how.

The groom and his merry men

A traditional black morning suit can look rather sombre at a wedding, so either brighten it up with stripy trousers, or opt for metallic silver or navy suits with a splash of colour in the form of plums and purples for the ties, or whatever colour links in with the bridesmaids or flowers. Some interesting ideas for men who don't want to wear morning suits include:

- Top hat and tails.
- His uniform, if he is in the police or armed forces.

- His national dress, that is, a kilt if he's Scottish, for example.

- A white suit (for the self-assured).

- A linen pastel lounge suit, with contrasting shirt.

- Black tie with cummerbund and bow tie.

- A bespoke pinstripe suit à la Paul Smith.

The group can make their outfits unique by adding special touches, such as a fob watch, personalised cufflinks (which match his watch), a cane, handkerchief, necktie, braces, socks, sunglasses – the only rule to remember is to keep shoes clean, lean and classic. Also, what about buying the group some matching, joke boxer shorts, with perhaps picture of you, the national flag or their names printed on them?

NB Ushers and the fathers of the groom and bride should replicate what the main man is wearing. Too many different styles of suit will look hideous in the photos. But to make the groom feel a little more special, he should wear a patterned necktie, or a waistcoat, and he could also wear a different, complementary colour of scarf/hankie, and so on. He should also wear a big badge saying 'groom'. No, he shouldn't really – he should simply have a more impressive buttonhole and pair of cufflinks.

The most unique groom I ever saw was one who'd got a Union Jack jacket made for the evening reception. Very cool Britannia. The most unusual usher I ever saw was one wearing a lion-tamer's red jacket and skin-tight breeches. It was not a good look – avoid at all costs.

Don't push your man into being too unusual in his dress though, or the only thing unique about your day will be a miserable groom and a group of drunken friends taking the mickey out of him. As the bride, you should provide the majority of the drama and glamour – it's wasted on a man.

Don't forget about our favourite male style icon, David Beckham. He grew a suave moustache and goatee beard especially for his wedding; and in the evening, he and his new bride changed into striking purple ensembles designed by top fashion guru, Antonio Berardi.

The bridesmaids

Ah, forget the rules about dressing your girls dowdily so you look better – you'll look and feel marvellous surrounding yourself with some gorgeous girls (and show what a cool, giving person you are at the same time!).

Long gone are the days when all the bridesmaids had to wear the same – regardless of their age and size. Now the key is making them feel comfortable and look beautiful.

A recent trend is to dress bridesmaids in different shades of the same colour. Another key to having them the same, yet different, is to put them all in the same dress but holding different bouquets or all in the same dress but of different lengths.

Ask your bridesmaids for ideas about what they'd like to wear – they're your best friends so they should have an idea what would suit them and please you. How about these styles:

- Prom queens – mini-cardigans, flared skirts and corsages.

- Red-carpet divas – long and slinky, and bright silks.

- Twinkle toes – sequins and sparkle, iridescent fabrics.

◆ Frills 'n' thrills – floaty chiffon and layering.

◆ 1960s sirens – belted dresses, chignons and kohl make-up.

Add a little extra to the theme by coordinating the accessories: dragonfly brooches, butterfly hair-slides, chandelier earrings, sequined pouch bags, and so on.

Bouquets should be in a complementary colour to yours, but not as large (the balance will be wrong). If you don't want your bridesmaids to have bouquets, try:

◆ Corsages, tied around the wrist or neck with matching ribbon.

◆ Get them to hold a single flower each.

◆ Give them matching fans or parasols.

◆ Matching clutch bags will look elegant.

◆ Flower hoops are sweet for the young, in the country.

BELLA, 29

❝ My six adult bridesmaids were all different shapes and sizes, so I stole an idea I'd found in a magazine. I chose a fabric, bought rolls and rolls of it and handed it out amongst them with my blessing to do what they wanted. I had no idea what they'd look like, and I got as much excitement out of watching them descend my parents' staircase in their gear as I got from looking at myself in the mirror. One had made a miniskirt and halter neck, another a big blancmange. It was a really fun, bonding experience and, because the colour and pattern was the same throughout the group, it looked interesting yet fine. ❞

The mother of the bride

What does the mother of the bride wear to look perfect (it's probably the best day of her life, bar her own wedding) without upstaging the bride? Well, she should talk to the bride: what colour does the bride think would complement her dress and her mother's character and colouring? The bride's mother should go shopping with the bride (perhaps when they are already out looking for a wedding dress) and try on different styles and shades.

Do

1. Wear a stunning hat – it will automatically say who you are.

2. Choose a block colour – patterns are too busy.

3. Wear one piece of amazing jewellery, a spectacular brooch, for example.

4. Tie in shoes, hat and handbag to complement the dress/suit.

5. Get hair and make-up done professionally to feel extra special.

Don't

1. Wear a tiara – far too princessy.

2. Wear white or ivory – that's for the bride.

3. Wear a miniskirt or a boob tube – elegance is key.

4. Try to be the centre of attention – the bride will be.

5. Get tied down with a sombre suit – if a dress is appropriate, wear it.

> **NB On the day before her wedding,** Hollywood actress Kate Beckinsale and her mother were spotted wearing 'Bride-to-be' and 'Mother of the bride' sequined tracksuit tops. Think about getting something similar printed up for your mum!

The congregation

Whatever the bride, groom and attendants wear sets the theme for your wedding. And for many couples, this may be as far as you need or want to go. But depending on the theme, it may be fairly easy to extend it to your wedding party, too. Be careful, though. Does your dad really want to be decked out like a Spanish matador or a Russian Cossack when he walks you down the aisle? Asking the guests to follow your idea is even more difficult, as you have no idea what spin they may put on your theme. Some safe bets to make your wedding unusual but not a disaster include:

◆ Black tie for all the men, cocktail dresses for the women.

◆ Pick a colour. Black or white are easiest, à la David and Victoria Beckham at their Irish wedding, or guests could wear one item that is the same colour as your husband's favourite football team's shirt, or your bridesmaids' dresses.

◆ Pick a period. 1920s flappers look glam; 1950s knee-length dresses are sweet, for example.

◆ State 'Lounge suits and casual cool' on invitations for a laidback wedding.

- Elton John has a 'white tie and tiara' party every year – make your day the same.

- Julia Roberts had a 'must wear denim' wedding, and the guests danced until dawn.

- To run a theme through the congregation, hand out buttonholes and corsages.

- Fancy dress?! You couldn't, could you?

Well, if your nearest and dearest think it's a good idea and you've always dreamt of a fantasy wedding, do it. I've heard of some amazing themes extended to dress, and the pictures – and parties – were amazing, too. Try:

- Romantic couples from history (Romeo and Juliet, Bonnie and Clyde, and so on).

- Oscar winners (an excuse to get out the diamanté and long dresses).

- Kings and Queens (Cleopatra, Henry VIII, Queen Victoria).

- The Roman Empire (men wear military, women wear togas and flowers).

- Titanic – turn-of-the-century style.

- Valentines – guests wear pink, red and hearts.

- Club Tropicana – Hawaiian shirts, flowers, grass skirts.

NB Avoid vicars and tarts, pimps and hookers, black and white minstrels, and anything else that could cause offence or embarrassment. Also, don't get upset if people get the theme wrong, or don't make the effort. Some people find the idea of dressing up mortifying. I've thrown dozens of fancy dress parties over the years and there are always a few friends who show up in top-to-toe black with a sour expression on their faces. Don't let it wind you up. If anything, they'll feel like the odd ones out – they don't need you making them feel bad.

Going-away gear

If you're leaving for your honeymoon on the night of the wedding, travelling in your wedding dress is very impractical and you may want to change into something more sensible. If your departure is going to be a public affair, you won't want to do what I did and board the plane in a tracksuit and with a ponytail. You'll want the last memory of you to be of a stunning lady of the world. Here's how:

◆ Remove heavy make-up, but re-apply mascara and lip gloss.

◆ Brush hair out of a fancy style and wear it loose with a clip.

◆ Take off your killer heels and wear the shoe du jour – be it Birkenstock sandals, Scholl clogs, Frye boots.

◆ Combine comfort and cool in a well-made suit or towelling tracksuit.

◆ To avoid wrapping up in an airline blanket, take a cashmere cardi or pashmina.

The last thing to do before you leave the party is to seek out the people who have made it all possible – your parents, his parents, your attendants – and say a special goodbye, then hurl your bouquet at the gaggle of crazy women, and hopefully climb elegantly into your waiting mode of transport (where your well-packed, well-planned suitcases should be waiting).

Secrets of success

◆ As soon as you get engaged, start ripping out pages of wedding, fashion and celebrity magazines. Steal ideas and make a pack of the dresses and styles you like so that you can take it shopping with you. Whenever a celebrity ties the knot, take a look to see if there are any elements of her style that you'd like to incorporate into your own wedding outfit.

◆ If you're really torn between two dresses, one flamboyant and another that is more reserved, buy both, if you can afford to. It could be fun to have two dream dresses and change into the more reserved one in the evening – it may be easier to dance in, too!

◆ Don't over-accessorise – and don't match every colour and style precisely. It will look contrived and formal.

◆ Remember who you are! If you're casual by nature, don't go prim. If you live and die in T-shirts why should your wedding day be different? Get your favourite shape made in silk, or add sequins.

◆ If you're going for a short and sexy wedding dress, don't put your bridesmaids in something long and formal – you'll look too frivolous by comparison.

◆ Large department stores and designer boutiques offer free

personal shopping advice, and beauty counters offer free makeovers. Make the most of them, and even try visiting a few if you want alternatives.

◆ If your groom is wearing a white bow tie with his tuxedo, you could wear one as a choker. Very Playboy bunny!

◆ This is your wedding day. If you're feeling at all self-conscious about anything, fix it. You need to feel 100 per cent. Get your teeth whitened, your lips plumped, your wrinkles botoxed – just do it carefully.

◆ Give your guests a dress code if you think they'll follow it. As I said, Posh and Becks told everyone to wear black and white, and the pictures looked stunning. But make sure you state the rules clearly on the invitation, and if you're demanding a special theme, put details in the envelope about where they could find these outfits.

◆ If you're thinking black tie, your wedding should be semi-formal and in the evening, not in a village hall at midday; the dress code should suit the surroundings.

◆ In Germany, wearing the flower myrtle in your headdress is a sign of good marital luck – and it's very pretty, too.

◆ When you've finished with your dress you have a number of options. You can sell it – and get some cash towards your next marvellous outfit. You can customise it: dye it, cut it, add bits to it, and so on. Or you can keep it for old times' sake, or for your daughter to wear. If you want to do this, go to a specialist cleaner and storage expert – you don't want it eaten by moths.

◆ As a special keepsake, ask your dress designer to give you her initial drawings and notes to frame. Give them to your mother or hang them in the downstairs loo.

Chapter Five

Glamorous gourmet

MORE THAN ANYTHING ELSE, food sets the right mood. This is where the majority of your budget will go, so make sure you're getting it right and getting what you really want. Go to your reception venue for a tasting session, and take along the parents and in-laws for a full run-through of the wedding breakfast menu a month before to check that everything is delicious. Don't feel forced to follow the safe route of soup, chicken and chocolate – but do offer alternatives for people with dietary requirements, and perhaps offer a choice if the venue – and your pocket – can accommodate a wider menu.

To dine or not to dine – a modern dilemma

With the prices of weddings going up by the hour, many people have come to the conclusion that a sit-down meal or buffet is an unnecessary expense. And don't fret if you agree! Simply hold your wedding at 5.00 p.m., and follow the service with a cocktail 'n' canapé soirée which lasts no longer than two hours – you can use the excuse of rushing off on your honeymoon. People have very busy lives and may even appreciate that your wedding doesn't take up their whole weekend.

Another idea is to go for an early-bird special – get married at 9.00 a.m. and follow it by a real 'wedding breakfast'. Persuade your favourite, nearby restaurant to open early for you, or make your way to an amazing hotel. Make it traditional – with a full English fry up or kippers and poached eggs, or a bit more glam with eggs Benedict or waffles. Having a wedding breakfast will not only save you money on the catering but also not too many people will be demanding cocktails before midday. Perhaps just serve Buck's Fizz or Bloody Marys.

If you really can't afford anything too fancy, just hold a special meal for your very nearest and dearest on the day, and hire a nightclub or bar soon after to celebrate with all and sundry, advising them that it won't be a free bar (perhaps just provide a DJ and some finger food). Decent people appreciate how expensive weddings are and won't moan.

Options for a high budget wedding

Make a meal out of it. For a memorable meal you will need to design the menu for your 'wedding breakfast' (as it is traditionally known). When you do this analyse every taste, texture and colour that your guest will be confronted with as they dine. Don't, for example, serve tomato soup, spaghetti bolognaise and strawberry mousse – everything is too red and saucy. Think of the meal as a whole, each course as important as the other. And as much as it's your day, don't be selfish in this one aspect; you may love venison but the majority of your guests won't. Be original, don't be inedible.

I was lucky enough to be a bridesmaid at a wedding at Claridges, London, where the impressive wedding meal was designed by super-chef Gordon Ramsay. The friends holding their wedding there valued good food and wine above all other aspects of their wedding – they'd been to too many dire dos which had left them starving and miserable. The idea – and the cost – paid off. The meal was beautifully presented and delicious, and everyone felt like royalty. There is definitely a shift in wedding priorities towards making the meal exciting and memorable. At another recent wedding I went to in the Essex countryside, the couple went off menu and spent a lot of money developing a meal that would look stunning and wow their guests. The meal is very much the heart and soul of a wedding, so don't just look at planning it as a chore to get your guests fed and watered. The meal can make or break a wedding.

Cool canapés

Just the idea of serving canapés is decadent and luxurious, something we're more used to hearing about at celebrity parties and royal weddings than at our own. But this is changing; in the last year, more weddings I've had the honour of being invited to have served them than not – and guests adore them. It's an unexpected extra that makes guests feel well taken care of. If you can afford to serve these bitesize delicacies, make sure:

1. There are between four to six per person if served before dinner, 12 if served as the main food.

2. They can be eaten in one mouthful.

3. The waiters serving also offer napkins.

4. There is a good mixture of meat, fish and vegetarian.

5. That the serving staff can explain to guests what is in each morsel.

6. That the serving staff work the room properly, and that a greedy bunch hanging around the kitchen door aren't getting them all.

7. That they look beautiful; a silver tray is elegant but I've been to some parties recently where the canapés have been served on ice, glass, mirrors, leaves, flowers, and in birdcages and baskets. Be creative with their display.

JESS, 35

❝ We'd booked our dream honeymoon to Mauritius, somewhere I'd always wanted to go. So we decided to prepare for the trip – and inspire others – by adapting our wedding menu to our voyage of a lifetime. I researched recipes and menus from Mauritian hotels and restaurants, and gave our chef clear instructions. Guests were greeted with waiters holding trays of fruit cocktails, which were a great success. We started the meal with a clear crayfish soup, then had baked fish with spinach and potato, followed by a tropical fruit cocktail. And to finish off? A cake in the shape of a desert island, complete with palm tree and us two on sun-loungers! ❞

The bread basket

Now, there are very few wedding guides that would put such emphasis on le pain – but I think it's important. In fact, the quality of the bread is one of the ways I judge how good a restaurant is. And at a wedding, when guests have been waiting, watching and drinking for hours, the bread rolls will go down quicker than a granny on a frosty morning. So make it tasty, don't just chuck a clump of doughy brick on to a side plate.

◆ Try different flavours (basil, olive, tomato, cheese, rosemary, poppy seed, sunflower seed, walnut, pine nut).

◆ Try different types (granary, wholemeal, baguette, bagels, cholla, toast, ciabatta, focaccia, flatbreads, naan, sourdough, pitta).

◆ Try serving with: balsamic vinegar and olive oil mixed, flavoured vinegar, herb-infused olive oil, thousand island dressing, lemon-scented butter, pâté, onion marmalade, quince, assorted chutneys, sour cream.

And don't stick to boring rolls – experiment with shapes. I went to a wedding where the centrepiece of each table was a tree made out of bread. Guests could break off branches and dip it in butter. I've been to another elegant soiree where, instead of a plate, guests ate off of a slice of unleavened loaf, constantly munching through the bread and the assorted dips during the whole meal.

NB Don't use the guidelines below just for your wedding day, follow them when hosting your first 'married' dinner party and other special evenings at home when you're serving food.

Starting position

This is the introduction to the feast, so it should be impressive. I don't mean in size – after all this is just the appetiser – but in colour, taste and originality. Even the plainest soup can be souped-up with a drizzle of olive oil and a sprig of fresh herbs. A simple salad can be turned into a work of art if served on the right crockery with a flamboyant swirl of dressing. Melon can be cut into interesting shapes and decorated with tropical fruits and flowers.

If you don't want the traditional, there are many more inspiring starters that stand out from the crowd:

♦ Oysters: served in piles on crushed ice with wedges of lemon, or in shot glasses with tomato juice and black pepper. Have pretty pots of sea salt and cracked black pepper on each table.

♦ Meze: instead of starter crockery, use flatbread as a plate and indulge in humus, tsatsiki, taramasalata, vine leaves and feta cheese salad.

♦ Antipasti: decorate the table with plates of salamis, hams, carpaccio, cheeses and roasted vegetables. Place decorative bottles of balsamic vinegar and olive oil on the table.

♦ Canapés: miss out on the sit-down bit for the first course, and serve melon, strawberries, mushroom tarts and prawn brioche as your guests mingle.

♦ Food cocktails: fill sundae glasses with your favourite seafood and salad, and drizzle with suitable sauces.

♦ Serve a cheese soufflé: these can get tricky if you have many guests, but are a well-received work of art if you are having a meal for a lucky few.

♦ Asparagus spears with a side jug of melted butter or hollandaise sauce is effortlessly elegant.

♦ A hearty warming soup's not hot stuff on a sticky, summer's day. Go for chilled gazpacho, with sour cream and chopped chives in the middle.

♦ Freshly baked mini-quiches for each individual, served on a bed of rocket.

♦ Forget a Greek salad, go the whole way and bake rounds of goat's cheese and serve them with fresh figs and a drizzle of raspberry vinegar.

> **NB You don't have to have a starter.** A cousin who wanted a traditional English wedding meal opted out of the first course and indulged her guests in sausages and mash, and apple pie ... and then cheese and biscuits with port as the third and final course.

The main deal

The 'main' thing to remember here is: don't be tight. Your guests have travelled, sat, followed, clapped, complimented; keep their spirits up with some proper, filling grub. Don't cut costs here, otherwise everyone will flag and leave early to grab a kebab on the way home.

♦ Surf and turf – dish out a tender steak with half a lobster or some giant prawns.

♦ Fillet steak with a side order of chunky chips is a meat-lover's favourite.

♦ If you and your friends love a good Ruby Murrey – serve curry. Avoid the super hot and spicy; instead serve each guest with a meat, fish or vegetable thali. This is a traditional dish, which means everyone gets a bit of everything, served individually so no one goes without. Rice, breads and bhajis are included.

◆ Salads are rarely served at weddings, but on a hot day there's nothing nicer than a fresh, well-made Caesar, or a warm steak and red onion combo.

◆ A roast dinner is always a winner – get the waiting staff to carve at each table. Don't forget the trimmings (Yorkshire puddings, chipolatas wrapped in bacon, fresh horseradish).

◆ Go 'old school' with toad in the hole, steak and kidney pie or bangers and mash.

◆ Beef on a bed of mash and spinach, with a red wine jus is instantly warming.

◆ Don't serve a boring chicken breast – stuff it with apple, mozzarella, pancetta or sun-dried tomatoes and make an interesting gravy in a complementary flavour.

◆ For a Friday wedding, grilled Dover sole with lemon sauce is traditional 'n' tasty, or creamy fish pie is comforting.

◆ Cuisine from the 1970s is making a comeback – duck à l'orange will raise a smile, as well as being tasty.

NB Side orders should be plain if the dish is fussy (spinach, new potatoes, glazed carrots, minted peas) and more extravagant if the main dish is simple (cauliflower cheese, peas mixed with ham, roasted parsnips, garlic mash).

Don't forget the veggies! No stuffed peppers should be on your menu – that's the epitome of naffness (and they don't taste very nice). Investigate mushroom stroganoff, vegetable laksi, noodles, risottos, pastas ... just not nut loaf! And of course, don't forget the kids – do something suitable, be it plainer/smaller versions of the adult meal, or a perennial favourite like fish fingers and peas. Make sure they have something to munch on while the adults tuck in to the starters – or you'll get wailing and little fingers in the food.

Just desserts?

All good things come to those who wait. For those with a sweet tooth this is the highlight of the meal. Make it a climax to remember. Or if you're especially proud of your wedding cake, get the cutting over and done with and serve a cheese course or petits fours. If you're going for a perfect pudding, however:

◆ Forget dry fruit cake, serve ice cream sundaes: go OTT with fruits and sweets, sprinkles and sauces. The kids (of all ages) will love it.

◆ A new trend is to hire a chocolate fountain machine. Warm cocoa cascades down different layers as guests can prod and poke marshmallows and cookies into its stream.

◆ The fine chocolatier, Godiva, makes a beautiful centre-piece designed as a lotus flower, which can double as dessert. Made entirely of chocolate, each leaf can hold different sweets and bonbons. Don't place it near the radiators, though.

◆ Set up a chocolate fondue on each table, and serve each guest with a plate of delicacies for dipping.

◆ Serve nibble-sized desserts, and give everyone a platter with a few to taste. A friend had the wonderful idea to serve a raspberry sorbet, champagne shot, crème brûlée and a chocolate biscuit on a rectangular plate – it tasted and looked amazing.

◆ If in doubt, go super-duper traditional: think sticky toffee pudding, apple and blackberry crumble, spotted dick, Eve's pudding, rice pudding – yum yum.

◆ The most wonderful wedding dessert I've ever had was chocolate soup (yes, warm and wet and utterly delicious) with a dollop of black pepper ice cream (yes, spicy and potent). The combination is like heaven on earth.

◆ Forget the browning fruit salad in syrup; get exotic: kiwi, mango, star fruit and papaya in natural juices are tangy and tasty.

◆ Crêpe Suzette flipped at the table add drama and excitement.

◆ Tarte tatin with cinnamon ice cream is easy and simple – and everyone loves it.

NB If you need to save some cash, serve your wedding cake as dessert – simply add ice cream, or leave jugs of cream on each table.

The finishing touches

Guests will expect coffee – go for filter if the venue can provide it. People will be too full to fancy a cappuccino or latte, but espresso could be a nice touch, especially if you want people to stay up late dancing, so investigate your options. Some people will ask for tea, or don't drink caffeine, so a thoughtful add-on would be to have a waiter walking the room with hot water and a selection of peppermint, camomile and raspberry infusions as well as having decaffeinated coffee available. This is a cheap treat, but feels very modern and classy.

At this point, it could be nice to serve truffles, petits fours, biscotti, and even chocolate Hobnobs (it sounds ridiculous, but they're everyone's favourite, and that's what counts). For the ultimate in kitch fun, serve Ferrero Rocher.

Make a gingerbread house stuffed with sweets for each table, for guests to nibble on with coffee, and finish off the meal with Cuban cigars and cognac.

If something savoury is desired, cheese is delicious – but no rubbery Cheddar and dry cream crackers, please, brides-to-be. For a little bit more money, the venue can serve a flavoured Stilton, a locally produced hard cheese, and a soft goat's cheese; go to your local deli and ask what they can supply to your venue. Instead of grapes and a curly bit of celery, try figs, prunes, pineapple, apple chutney, onion marmalade and tomato relish.

Sweet treats

When your guests start to feel peckish, they may not want another course of stodgy food, so bring them sweetness and light with:

◆ Mini-ice cream cones in assorted flavours, with a self-service bar for extras such as flakes, sprinkles and marshmallows.

◆ Champagne-flavoured ice lollies, on personalised sticks.

◆ Fresh cream cakes served with strawberries with sprinklers and candles.

◆ Individual jellies in decorative cups, served with jugs of cream.

◆ A variety of alcohol-laced fudges and toffee squares.

ARE YOU BEING SERVED – PROPERLY?

Anyone that's eaten out before will know that even the finest dinner can be ruined by poor service. Introduce yourself to the head waiter and maître d' before your big day. Be friendly and respectful, and even offer a cash tip at the end of the meal if all goes well. Sure, it's a bribe – but it's your big day. Checkpoints to remember:

1. Ascertain the staff-to-guest ratio – it should be between 1:10 and 1:20.

2. Make sure there is bar staff at all times, in case guests wish to buy their own drinks instead of the wine provided with the meal.

3. Point out the special table or guests so that they receive service first.

4. Matching cutlery and crockery is a must-have.

5. What will the serving staff be wearing? At the very least it should be of similar styles, that is white shirts and black skirts or trousers. For extra panache, why not get special T-shirts printed for them to wear while they're serving dinner? Decorate them with a favourite picture and the date on the front, and the wedding breakfast menu on the back.

6. Let the head waiter know there will be a healthy tip at the end of the night if food arrives quickly, warm and without much spillage. I fully advocate bribery on wedding days!

Options for a medium budget

Bootilicious buffets

If you're determined not to spend all your cash on food, opt for a buffet. If you're affluent, or feeling hungry, have a meal and serve a buffet three hours later – which will be perfect for your evening guests. Hungry dancers and drinkers will descend on your offering like Pavarotti in a parachute, so make sure you have enough. It really will be eaten. Delicious, easy and cheaper than a sit-down meal, here are some great ideas.

◆ Deli style is cool for a laidback New York City feel. Stack up plates of hot dogs, pastrami sandwiches and cookies plus bowls of potato chips and coleslaw. Serve with obligatory ice-cold beer and Coca-Cola. Would root beer and ice cream soda be too much? Never – it's your wedding day.

◆ Mamma mia! Bellisimo. Everyone loves Italian. An easy buffet, especially good for the summer, includes bruschetta, garlic bread and pizzas with mozzarella and tomato salads. Pasta may be too much, but if your guests are big eaters …

◆ A French farmers' market will add some *je ne sais quoi*. Lay out platters of cheeses (each with little flags offering the name and description) surrounded by strawberries and kiwi, crêpes and croque-monsieur sandwiches.

◆ If you have a sweet tooth, this is your day to indulge it. Serve a plethora of cakes, pastries, gateaux, ice creams, sorbets, mousses and pies. Make sure there's plenty of custard, cream, crème fraîche and fromage frais too.

◆ Go Mexican – it's hot, sexy and easy to prepare. Think nachos, enchiladas, salads and rice. It can be left all night without losing its flavour (and tastes extra good washed down with beer 'n' lime or tequila.

◆ Go back to your childhood – serve triangle sandwiches, cheese and pineapple sticks, mini-sausages, with colourful napkins and paper plates.

◆ Seafood stalls. My sister-in-law and brother-in-law had this at their recent wedding and the over-30s went crazy for it. Served on a traditional East End-style market stall, bowls and platters of *fruits de mer* nestled on beds of ice – it was the highlight of the evening. Cockles, mussels, prawns, calamari – sure you're asking for a bout of food poisoning, but use good suppliers and keep it at the right temperature and you'll become a wedding buffet legend.

◆ BBQs just say summer! Burgers and hot dogs are fabulous, grilled halloumi and spicy chicken kebabs with toasted pitta breads are even better. Side dishes of coleslaw, baked beans, gherkins, potato salad and fried onions will make this an easy – and reasonably priced – fiesta of the taste buds.

◆ Fondue fancies: set out platters of toast, ham and vegetables to dip into melted cheese.

◆ Not got loads of cash for a buffet? Set up a sandwich bar. Get one member of staff to set up a table with a basket of baguettes and a selection of fillings.

> ### HIGH TEA
>
> Another medium-to-low budget binge is to serve tea. Think Miss Marple at the Ritz. Serve cups of Earl Grey or Long Island iced tea, with cucumber sandwiches, fairy cakes and vol-au-vents. How classy! Set the grub out on silver platters and dine with fine bone china.

Options on a small budget

Cheap treats

If you want to feed and water your guests adequately but are worried about the cost, there are a few simple cost-cutters.

1. Make it a BYOB party – bring your own bottle.

2. Take your own booze to the venue and pay only corkage (go directly to a wine warehouse, vineyard or to the Continent for cheap-and-cheerful wine).

3. Save on staff by making the buffet and bar self-service.

4. Have a BBQ; they instantly put people in a party mood and won't cost a fortune. Keep to burgers, sausages, baked potatoes and salads.

5. Bake your own wedding cake, or if you can't go to that, get a plain shop-bought one and ask a clever friend to ice it for you. Or buy fairy cakes from your local bakers and pile them high to make a stunning scene for the photos. Instead of cutting a cake, you can simply eat one!

6. If people offer to help, accept it with gratitude.

7. Hold your wedding at 5.30 p.m., and on your invitations simply state 'Guests are welcome to join the couple for a

celebratory drink'. Go to the local pub or wine bar and put whatever you can afford behind the bar.

8. Hold the wedding breakfast at home: get in local caterers and buy the booze from the supermarket – there's no corkage fee at home!

9. Spaghetti can be a lifesaver – and everyone loves it! Make it special by serving heart-shaped pasta with tomato sauce and fresh basil.

10. Cook and freeze dishes, and then reheat them on the day. Ask friends to store things for you. Even canapés such as mini-quiches can be frozen.

11. Buy a small, elaborate cake for the pictures, then serve a larger, cheaper version to guests instead of dessert.

12. If your heart is set on champagne for the toasts, buy magnums rather than normal-sized bottles – it will work out slightly cheaper.

13. If you're whining about the cost of wine, forget bottles and stock up on boxes instead. The contents aren't as bad as is sometimes believed, and if you're worried about them looking ugly, allow the wine to breathe or cool in carafes.

Crème de la crème of cakes

The three-tiered fruit cake is nice (sometimes!) but the traditional reason for having such a thing (so that it lasts for the christening of the first child) is pretty much redundant these days. So feel free to experiment with lemon, orange, chocolate, carrot, nut, ice cream, profiteroles and cheesecakes. Why not have a different flavour for each tier? A friend did this most successfully at her recent wedding, and it's the first time I haven't seen any left over at the end of the evening.

What you put on top of the cake is a different matter; you can go kitsch and forget about good taste altogether. Why not have a mini-bride and groom placed on top (and in Scandinavia it's good luck to hide a model baby up the bride's dress!). Ask a local artist to make mini versions of you both. Or if you're going on the honeymoon of a life-time, have suitcases on top, or decorate the cake with animals if you're going on a safari. If you want to keep it simple but special, invest in some edible glitter or fluorescent icing.

I rebelled at my wedding, and each guest got a fairy cake decorated with symbols that meant something to my new husband and me: our teams' football shirts, our national flags, the date of our wedding, and so on. These were moist and tasty – and talked about for a long time after. Simple cup cakes in chocolate and orange, iced and sprinkled with hundreds and thousands are lovely.

Allow guests to take home their slice of wedding cake by providing personalised, pretty cake boxes or bags. Place them near to the exits so that guests don't forget.

NB A new craze – especially in anti-sugar California – is to have a savoury wedding cake. A three-tier goat's cheese terrine decorated with peppers, tomato and asparagus spears looks simply stunning – and a surprisingly good accompaniment to dessert wines and cocktails. Good caterers will be able to do this for you.

Drink to the future!

Weddings are an excuse to get romantic, silly and emotional, and, sadly, when we're all so used to keeping a stiff upper lip in our day-to-day lives, most of us need a few beverages to loosen up (and cry during the speeches, and dance all night, and tell everyone you love them ...). In that respect, choosing the booze is a very important factor when planning a wedding. What you serve and how you serve it can really set the tone. So if you fancy being a little more experimental than serving lukewarm sparkling wine, don't get shaken and stirred! There are economical ways of splashing out the drink at your wedding.

A day of drinking

Before the ceremony
It's not your duty to supply drinks before the service (and certainly not during). If the groom invites others to meet him for drinks an hour before, he should be prepared to buy everyone a drink – but more often than not they'll be buying his Dutch courage for him. Brides: steer clear of anything too heavy (or that can stain your dress) until after all your pictures have been taken.

After the ceremony
In many ways this is the most crucial time. Guests can get bored and the day can lose momentum, so keep it going by serving cool, beautiful drinks, and plenty of them. Budget for three glasses of whatever per person.

During the meal
It is normal to supply half a bottle of wine per guest during the meal, but if you want to serve more, it will be welcome.

Don't dare double the quantities by halving the quality of the vino, though – you'll be left with lots of pongy vinegar at the end of the night and the guests won't be merry. On a table of 10 people, put out three bottles of white and two of red wine – there are usually more white drinkers than red. Remember to put bottles of water on the table, too. If you're saving cash, don't worry about buying bottled water – serve jugs of iced water with slices of lemon or lime.

After-dinner extras
My cousin left bottles of port on each table to enjoy with a selection of cheeses at her wedding – it was a unique touch that left everyone feeling spoilt (if a little worse for wear the next morning). Other favoured after-dinner tipples are brandy, cognac, Bailey's, Kahlúa. If you can't afford to leave a bottle on each table (after all, some people won't fancy it), ask a waiter to walk around with a tray of individual shots. A digestif such as Limoncello works well at this time.

For the speeches
Champagne, if you can afford it, is always a treat. Serve the pink variety if it matches your wedding colours. This can prove pricey, so investigate the British and Spanish sparkling wines, which really aren't awful. Just make sure they're served at the right temperature in the right glasses. And never touch Babycham or Asti Spumante … too sweet and fizzy.

NB Champagne is expensive so when serving it make sure the long-stemmed glasses are clean and free from detergent (which will damage the bubbles) and that the bottles are pointed away from guests when they are opened. I've seen a waiter fire the cork in the pianist's eye, which was certainly unique but not in the right way. It should be served no colder than eight degrees.

Cocktail hour

Keep things fun and fruity with some cooling cocktails. A gin or vodka concoction can often work out cheaper than a glass of good wine. You can make them in advance so that guests can grab a glass on arrival, but make sure they are sufficiently chilled. Try the old – and new – wedding classics: Buck's Fizz, Bellini, Kir Royale, Gin Fizz, Caipirinha, Mojito, Martini, Cosmopolitan, Pimms No. 1, and so on.

Have fun with the decoration: lace the rim of the glass with sugar or salt (if you're being very cool you can dye the sugar), slices of fruit, berries, physalis, straws, stirrers, hanging monkeys/palm trees, edible glitter sprinkled on the top, coloured ice, ice with fruit in it … and use the right style of glass.

Serve cocktails between the service and the wedding breakfast and allow for two each – there's nothing worse than moaning, parched guests. Don't serve cocktails after the meal: they are an aperitif and lose their allure after a heavy meal.

> **NB Need to cut back?** You'll save lots of money by asking the venue if you can bring your own booze. Or serve fizzy wine instead of champers for the toasts.

Shot to the heart

Long drinks are to be expected at elegant weddings, so dare to be different and warm up events with some shots. These mini-glasses of rocket fuel look stunning and can be downed and whisked away by the waiter within seconds. Try mini Bloody Marys, tequila with salt and lemon, vodka jellies, vodka-laced gazpacho, B52s, sambuca (on fire!). Just make sure there's plenty of water available, and don't serve them all night.

Sober thoughts

It's very boring being the designated driver or recovering alcoholic at a wedding, as it's normally the occasion when the most sensible person decides to let it all go, down too much booze and get the female relatives doing 'Agadoo'. Brighten up the non-drinkers restricted misery by at least serving more than water and a selection of slightly warm, flat soft drinks. Serve non-alcoholic cocktails (which are again cheap but tasty, and can be decorated to make up for the lack of liquor) or some inspired juices: freshly squeezed orange, carrot and apple or a berry smoothie will provide lots of flavour and interest. Whatever you do – remember them. I've been to too many weddings where the driver has had to leave the reception to find an outside bar, just to get a Diet Coke. And also remember to lay on lemonade and Coca-Cola, as well as other soft drinks, for the children.

> **MARIE, 32**
>
> ❛ People are always ready for a drink after the service, so while we're having our pictures taken, we're doing Pimms – it will look very pretty topped with fresh mint and strawberries. Men often don't like traditional wedding drinks, such as champers and Buck's Fizz, so we're ordering in special kegs of beer, and will set them up as a feature where the men can help themselves. ❜

Secrets of Success

◆ Make an entrance when you arrive for dinner. Ask the Master of Ceremonies/best man to announce 'Mr and Mrs Just-Marrieds' – or better still, follow a piper or violinist to your table.

◆ Sugar, sugar – how you thrill me! How about purchasing some romantic sugar cubes to serve with tea and coffee. Cox & Cox do very cute squares with red hearts on. Guaranteed to make grandmas ooh and ahh. You could also coat drink stirrers in caramel or sugar, or provide chocolate spoons.

◆ Fortune cookies are a great way to finish off a dinner. Produce a plate at the end of the meal and your guests will get a snack and a prediction. They can taste a little dry, so dip them in melted chocolate, sprinkle some hundreds and thousands over them and then leave them to set overnight.

◆ Don't feel tied to one food theme. If you love Italian cooking but your husband has Jamaican roots, mix and match. What's wrong with serving jerk chicken with a Caprese salad? Nothing!

◆ At her 30th birthday party, Kate Moss handed out specially made loveheart sweets inscribed with the words 'With love from Kate'. Do the same, perhaps with your names, or the date of the wedding, or some simple romantic sentiment ... how about your nicknames for each other? Guests will wonder who on earth 'Badger and Monkey' are – and you'll giggle about it all night.

♦ Give speeches a modern slant by either having them before the meal (that way nervous speakers can enjoy the food), perform a speech yourself or go Continental and not have speeches at all. Just allow anyone who wants to say a few words to stand up and take the microphone.

♦ Update the usual seating plan by having guests play musical chairs between courses or be informal and let guests sit where they want.

♦ If you can't afford a sit-down meal and the weather's nice, have a picnic: serve pastry foods, chunky sandwiches and seasonal fruits, with plenty of salads and ice-cold white wine.

♦ Offer your guests trays of mini-portions of fish and chips in newspaper cones.

♦ Supermodel Kristen McMenamy and Kate Winslet both organised trendy bangers and mash for their reception meal.

♦ Serve veggie and meaty mini-hamburgers at midnight – they're easy to eat, delicious and look cute. Pin them together with mini-flags representing where you and the groom are from, or where you are going on honeymoon. Serve bacon butties if the wedding celebration is going on until morning.

♦ Japanese style is still very in, so serve up sushi and sake at a cocktail party reception.

♦ Do a Posh and Becks and perch near-nude icing figures of you and your groom on top of your cake. Just use an iced fig leaf or two to save your blushes. And another tip from them: have his-and-her individual desserts. Their guests could choose between Victoria's favourite, summer berry terrine, or his, sticky toffee pudding. You can guess which was the most popular!

◆ Get rid of the fruit cake and serve a traditional French wedding cake: a croquembouche (a caramelised profiterole mountain), or have a novelty cake. I've seen football pitches and an Eiffel Tower.

◆ Don't be tied to tradition. If you want to serve a red wine with chicken, or you adore rosé and want all your guests to try it – do so!

◆ Ice, ice baby! For a summer wedding, nothing is nicer than beating the heat with a cool, long drink. Make it even more special by preparing special ice cubes – add food colouring, or fruit and berries, or tiny leaves and flowers, to the water and leave them to freeze. Another special idea for the evening is to buy those amazing battery-driven, illuminated ice cubes – they glow in different colours for a few hours at a time! Even Marks & Spencer sell them now!

◆ Lets drink to drink! Mini-bottles of champagne with straws are classy. If you're serving martinis – shaken not stirred – get the waiters to wear 007-style black tie. The ladies will love it. If you're having cocktails, treat guests to mixers and shakers at the bar – and as a take-home gift.

◆ Remember that the best celebrity bashes have an ice sculpture; serve drink through it and make it the centrepiece at your reception. Go for a model of you and the groom – or a simple ice mountain. It will be the talking point of the wedding.

◆ Add interest at the bar by leaving personalised matchboxes, ashtrays and stirrers.

◆ Dishes of olives and nuts go down well, too.

Chapter Six

Let me entertain you

|T COSTS PEOPLE A LOT OF MONEY to travel, get dressed up and buy presents for a wedding – so make sure they enjoy it buy laying on some marvellous entertainment. A wedding isn't just about commitment and true love. Oh no, having a jolly good party is a massive part of it, too!

Music mayhem

You don't have to stick with the classic cheesy DJ (you know the type: open Hawaiian shirt showing hairy chest and medallion), try something a bit more unusual:

- ◆ Hire a tribute band. If you love Abba, get a look-alike group who dress up and sing the same.

- ◆ Focus on a decade. Be it 1960s, 1970s, 1980s or 1990s – to give a real retro feel.

- ◆ Get a themed DJ. One who wears fancy dress and takes on a persona for the whole night, offering jokes and gifts in their style.

- ◆ If you've got a gaggle of musical mates, encourage them to form a band for the evening.

- ◆ Think about getting an impersonator to charm your guests all night.

- ◆ You don't have to do the full-on disco thing – think about hiring a harpist, pianist, string quartet, percussion band or swing band for a bit of class.

- ◆ Make your own party tapes, and then ask the venue for adequate sound systems and speakers. This really is music you control! And it's cheap!

- ◆ Hey, hire a celebrity. Robbie Williams sang at his secretary's wedding, and Kylie can be borrowed for an evening (for a large sum of course).

SARAH, 29

6 We'd been to a few weddings where the guests had sat in stony silence during the meal, or struggled to make small talk. We didn't want that, so we hired a Dean Martin impersonator who we'd seen on the tribute show *Stars in Their Eyes* to sing during our supper. He had all the chat, plus a

great voice, and he charmed our guests into singing and dancing with him. We had people swaying on their chairs before the desserts were served, which upset the catering manager but made the photographer's job much easier. And then my husband, a massive Dino fan, got up and sang a duet with him, and I honestly think that was the highlight of his whole day. 🔸

Music makes the people come together

Every expert party-thrower knows the key to a good do is picking the right music. If the pace isn't right, guests will sit down and get tired, or worse still, go home! From the moment guests arrive for the service until they leave at night, make it moving and original. Do remember to set up a quiet room where guests can chill out and chat, though.

Aisle be there

The scariest moment for any girl is when she turns up at the service and has countless pairs of eyes boring into her as she tries to steady her steps and make it to the top of the aisle into the embrace of her betrothed. Just remember that you do look beautiful, everyone is wishing you well, and it'll be over within a minute!

Take some of the pressure off yourself by walking in to some exquisite, unusual music. Some amazing tunes suitable for modern weddings include:

'Gabriel's Oboe', Ennio Morricone.

'I do, I do, I do', Abba.

'The Heart Asks Pleasure First', theme from *The Piano*.

'Faith, Hope and You', Phil Campbell.

'Nothing Fails', Madonna.

Ask friends with a talent to play their preferred instrument while you're signing the register, or think about a reprise of the tune you made your entrance to. If the church has a choir and bell ringers, make the most of them; the more music that fills a church, the better! You don't have to get them to stick to traditional hymns – if you take the music sheets early enough, and ask nicely, they may be able to learn your favourite song. The same applies to the organist: don't let it get gloomy – pick carefully.

To walk back down the aisle as husband and wife, you want something uplifting and celebratory, so let loose with a big, pompous concerto, your national anthem, the song your parents left the church to on their wedding day, or a raucous pop song, such as:

'Knew You Were Waiting (For Me)', Aretha Franklin and George Michael.

'My First, My Last, My Everything', Barry White.

'Let's Get Married', The Proclaimers.

'Together in Electric Dreams', Georgio Moroder and Phil Oakley.

'You're the One That I Want', John Travolta and Olivia Newton-John.

First impressions

In the build-up to your wedding day, one of the most frequently asked questions will be, 'What's your first dance going to be?' If you want to keep it a secret, don't feel pressured to share. Keep everyone guessing. If you're not precious about it, tell all, to gauge public opinion, but don't listen to those who don't like it if you're 100 per cent sure. On the day, make sure the DJ has the correct – and a good quality – version of the song. And make sure you and your newly betrothed are in the room when he announces the first dance. I've seen too many grooms have to dance with their mothers because the bride is busy gossiping in the toilets. Spice up the first dance a bit by inviting all the other married couples to join you for the second verse – and grab your parents for a quick dance and to catch up with each other before the evening gets under way.

Your first dance doesn't have to be slushy – it can be romantic, or cheesy, or fun and fast. Pick whatever you and your partner know you can make an impact with.

Romantic first dances

'By Your Side', Sade.

'Let's Stay Together', Al Green.

'The Way You Look Tonight', Elton John.

'The Way You Look Tonight', Frank Sinatra.

'Woman', John Lennon.

'Greatest Day', Beverley Knight.

'Something', The Beatles.

'Truly, Madly, Deeply', Savage Garden.

'It Had to Be You', Harry Connick Jnr.

'You Do Something to Me', Paul Weller.

Cheesy first dances

'The Time of My Life', Bill Medley and Jennifer Warnes.

'Tonight, Tonight', *West Side Story* (Leonard Bernstein).

'Solid', Ashford and Simpson.

'Save Your Love', Renee and Renata.

'Wonderful Tonight', Eric Clapton.

'Lucky Star', Madonna.

'Don't Go Breaking My Heart', Elton John and Kiki Dee.

'Especially For You', Kylie Minogue and Jason Donovan.

'Take On Me', Aha.

'Friday I'm in Love', The Cure (if marrying on a Friday!).

And to avoid at all costs:

'Lady in Red', Chris de Burgh (the bride's in white!).

'The Winner Takes it All', Abba (you'll sound smug).

'Satisfaction', The Rolling Stones (you'll sound frustrated).

'Careless Whisper', George Michael (you'll sound regretful).

'I Love Your Smile', Shanice (eurgh!).

'I'm Not in Love', 10CC (well, you should be!).

'Road to Nowhere', Talking Heads (could it be true?).

'Tragedy', The Bee Gees or Steps (both versions equally sad).

The current number one (too time sensitive).

And if you're very lucky, there may be a song named after you:

'Alice', Cocteau Twins.

'Alison', Elvis Costello.

'Amy', Ryan Adams.

'Angie', The Rolling Stones.

'Sweet Caroline', Paul Anka.

'Cecilia', Simon & Garfunkel/Suggs.

'Charlotte Sometimes', The Cure.

'Donna', Richie Valens.

'Emma', Hot Chocolate

'Gloria', Them.

'Iris', The Goo Goo Dolls.

'Isabel', Bjork.

'Sweet Jane', Velvet Underground.

'Julia', The Beatles.

'Julie', Shakin' Stevens.

'Laura', Scissor Sisters.

'Louise', Maurice Chevalier.

'Mandy', Barry Manilow/Westlife.

'Maria', Blondie.

'Michelle My Belle', The Beatles.

'Nancy', Frank Sinatra.

'Sexy Sadie', The Beatles.

'Sarah', Thin Lizzy.

'Victoria', The Kinks.

NB Make the most of your time in the spotlight.
Arrange with the venue to have balloons or glitter cascading
from the ceiling when you hit the dance floor. Or arm the
under-14s or the wedding party with streamers and party
poppers. Ask the DJ (or lighting engineer if you're so flash!)
to sort out a spotlight to focus on you, or some dazzling
lights to entice everyone on to the floor.

Karaoke kings

People have very different reactions to sing-a-long-a celebrations, but I love 'em. They are great icebreakers, and as
long as no one feels forced to stand up and sing, great fun
can be had by all. There'll always be the Celine's-in-waiting
who'll hog the microphone while others sit around, clap-
ping and enjoying the theatrics.

If you're going to have a karaoke theme at your wedding, provide enough song books to share around every
table – and make sure there's an up-to-date collection of
songs available, not just things from the Dark Ages. Finally,
make sure the microphone works, and try to arrange a
stage area to elevate the warbler above the crowd.

ANDREA, 29

❝ We decided to get married at my husband's old school, so really wanted an old-school day. Our first dance was a classic we loved when we were teenagers, and we hired a DJ who reminded us of nightclubs we visited when we were growing up. When our guests had worked up an appetite, we opened up a tuck shop, loaded with space hoppers, flumps and cola bottles, which we washed down with bottles of fizzy pop. We released sparkly confetti from the ceiling when we danced our last dance. ❞

Dancing Queens

Get the dancing going by:

- Hiring a professional dance caller to make sure everyone moves in time.

- Asking a dance teacher to get the party started with an hour of instruction.

- Setting a theme to get people going, for example, Morris dancing, a ceilidh or breakdancing.

- Getting a dance troupe in to do a mid-evening show wearing colourful costumes.

- Starting off the evening with the holiday classics ('La Bamba', 'La Macarena', 'Saturday Night', 'Superman', 'Agadoo', 'The Birdie Song'). They are tacky, but family weddings always are, and drunken aunties will go hell for leather!

◆ Hitting the dance floor yourself. If the bride and groom are having such fun they don't leave the dance floor, their guests will have to join them to say hello.

◆ Going all elegant with an evening of ballroom dancing, so you and the groom should have a few dance lessons beforehand to impress your nearest and dearest. If you don't fancy the safe-and-steady waltz and foxtrot, go for the salsa and samba.

◆ Starting a limbo competition or do the locomotion around the room to gather people in and keep them on the dance floor. The sit down classic 'Oops Upside Your Head' is another pull-'em-in favourite.

◆ Line dancing sounds naff, but it really can be fun. Get an instructor to lead you through an hour's worth of cowboy yeah-haws!

NB A fab wedding favour would be to make a CD or tape of the most memorable music of your reception, and present copies to the guests as they leave. Print a personalised case with the song titles and wedding details on it.

Save the last dance

So long, farewell, *auf Wiedersehen, adieu*! How does one bid au revoir to the best day of their life? Well, we don't shuffle backwards out of the door curtseying. Oh no, you've got to go out with a bang – a bigger bang than you walked in to the service all those hours ago in fact! And you're going to have to try even harder, because everyone is feeling a bit knackered and a little the worse for wear.

So the first rule is, you don't have to say goodbye to everyone – that will take you ages, and then if you miss out one poor sod, he'll take it personally. Instead:

- Jump up on stage, grab the microphone from the DJ and do a little speech of thanks and goodbyes.

- Arrange for your getting-away car to pull up outside the exit, run in to it, beep the horn and ask your ushers to shove everyone outside on to the kerb to watch you dash off into the night.

- Gather your guests into a big circle and link hands for 'Auld Lang Syne'.

- Everyone likes to cancan! Get the girls together for a big flash of thigh to 'New York, New York', while the men can down the pints and feel proud.

- Repeat your first dance, but this time with everyone hitting the floor.

Don't forget the golden oldies

Sing and dance surrounded by your nearest and dearest to 'close the show' with an all-time classic:

'My Way', Frank Sinatra.

'Perfect Day', Lou Reed.

'Unchained Melody', Righteous Brothers.

'Hey Jude', The Beatles.

'Edge of Heaven', Wham!

Thoroughly entertaining!

But let's not wish your night away ... there are plenty of other aspects to add to a fun and frantic evening:

Fireworks: these always make the night whiz by in a flash. Hand out sparklers to all your guests and hire a qualified pyrotechnic team to put on a dazzling display. Don't allow a family member who's had too much to drink to take over. If possible, tie in the finale to a favourite piece of music, and, if fireworks in your wedding colours exist, go for those too. If it's a chilly night, serve mulled wine, or Irish coffees to guests as they stand out to watch. If you're feeling flush, provide shawls or blankets as takeaway gifts that the ladies can wrap around themselves. Embroider your initials on to the corner to remind them where they got them.

People power: there is nothing funnier than watching your mates leap out of their skin when a living statue suddenly bursts to life! Hire these moving marble marvels to liven up the drinks reception and/or the line-up (which can be long and very dull!). Just make sure your granny doesn't take a peak under the man's fig leaf! Another fun thing to liven up the guests' entrance is to hire impersonators. I went to an American wedding with a look-alike of the Queen and people's reactions were fab. Think about getting your parents' favourite performers, or some lively 'infamous' types who'll cheer up proceedings. There are lots of these agencies around, bursting with the good, the bad and the ugly.

ART ATTACK

For instant appeal, and a take-home gift for your guests, hire an artist to walk around the tables and draw caricatures or silhouettes. Think about getting a balloon artist in for a laugh – even if he can only successfully make a sausage dog. Get an origami expert in to enthral your guests before the disco starts. On a different artistic bent, send round a poet to freestyle rap for your guests, and make up little ditties about them from a few chosen details. Have guests followed around by mime artists, mimicking their movements – much to everyone else's amusement.

Mystic magic: guests – and female guests in particular – will love the opportunity to get their palm read, or their future told from cards or a crystal ball. Set up a private area to the side of the dance floor where people can hear their dreams come true. Ask your psychic pal to dress up in the full garb for more atmosphere. Don't go so far as to hold mini-séances though – a wedding is neither the time nor the place, however much you wish grandpa could be with you.

Fairground attraction: if your venue has impressive grounds, and it's OK to bring things into them, think about hiring a mini-fairground. Of course dodgems is a must, although a rollercoaster is probably too cumbersome and impractical. Ghost trains, crooked houses, waltzers and merry-go-rounds are great for all ages – and of course, don't forget the coconut shy, apple-bobbing, shooting range and win-a-teddy fishing game. Set up stalls serving dough-nuts, candyfloss and popcorn.

GOOD SPORTS

Entertain your guests by setting up some sporting challenges. Arrange for a side room to have a dart board, table tennis and basketball hoops. Set up five-a-side football championships and games of rounders or baseball if the weather is good and the gardens are substantial enough. Cool everyone down with ice lollies and frozen margaritas.

Circus circus: all the world loves a clown, so get some big-footed fellas to walk round, trip over and squirt water at the serving staff. I wouldn't recommend you bring real animals in – too cruel – but a few pantomime-style horses with entertainers inside could be fun. Jugglers, acrobats and ringmasters can all whip the guests up into a frenzy of excitement.

Let's get quizzical

This is a new favourite thing to do at weddings: ask lots of questions, give out the answers, then the prizes, and then the insults! (all jokey, of course). Pub quizzes are growing in popularity, and as they do so, more brides and grooms are instigating them as icebreakers between guests, and fun things to liven up a dull half hour. Ask a loud friend or the master of ceremonies to play quiz master, and set out answer sheets and visual aids (and pens) on each table. Ask each group to think of a silly team name, or identify them by table names. The following topics are always popular:

◆ Guess what happened on the hen and stag nights.

◆ The wedding couple's history.

- School subjects, such as history, geography, art and so on.

- Music from each decade.

- Films and television.

- Famous catch phrases and last words.

- Famous couples throughout history.

Or try something more specific to your theme. If you're getting married at a football stadium, the blokes will be happy with a quiz on famous footballers. If you're getting married abroad, question your guests on the customs of the country you're in.

Child's play

Don't ignore the kids, whatever you do. Kids should behave themselves at weddings and the best way to ensure this happens is to keep them entertained. Set up a separate room with a child's entertainer in it, and lay out tables with non-toxic crayons, paper and stickers. If you find a good children's entertainer, they should be able to handle up to 12 kids on their own – and keep them happy by teaching them dance routines, putting on a puppet show, playing games or encouraging competitions. If the worst comes to the worst, and you really just want the parents – your friends – to have a good time, put the kids in a room with a television, a collection of DVDs and an au pair. This will give the parents a break.

Always remember, don't feel bad if your wedding is a child-free zone. Just state clearly on the invitation exactly who is invited, and don't weaken to demands that the kids really want to go to the wedding if you don't want them there. Weddings can be boring for kids and then they can become noisy and disruptive. It might be difficult for the parents to find a babysitter for the whole day (especially if they have to travel a long distance and would need to leave their children with someone overnight), or perhaps they can't imagine a day away from the whipper-snapper, but mostly, they could do with a bit of fun away from their kids as much as you could! If they cannot, or do not wish, to make the necessary arrangements for whatever reason, they may not be able to come. But it's your wedding and you should have it how you want it.

MOLLY, 35

❝ I'm the last of six daughters to get married, so by the time someone made an honest woman of me I had loads of nieces and nephews. I was torn between wanting them there and wanting them out of the way so my siblings could have a few drinks and relax. So, they came to the church and acted as flower girls and pageboys, and then they were whisked straight off to my oldest sister's house by three trusted childminders – and had a mini-wedding of their own. The kids got dressed up, had a dinner that suited them, had a mini-pop disco and too many sweets ... then got ushered upstairs and into their pyjamas. I paid the childminders extra to stay overnight so my sisters could stay at our hotel and get a weekend away out of it!'

Secrets of Success

◆ For a hot and steamy summer wedding, celebrate the great outdoors with some traditional holiday entertainment: get the crowds up for a limbo contest; hula dancers are colourful; fire eaters are exciting; samba or steel bands are sexy. Set up some paddling pools to cool down after a few drinks, and erect a bouncy castle. Set up a game of five-a-side football, cricket, or a tug-of-war.

◆ Russell Crowe had an Aboriginal fertility rite performed at his wedding. And it certainly worked – his wife had a baby shortly afterwards. This could add a mystic element to proceedings.

◆ If finding a perfect DJ is proving difficult, hire a jukebox instead. Fill it with your favourite tracks from a few different decades to keep everyone happy.

◆ Do you have lots of keen nieces, nephews or cousins who would love to put on a kids' show? Ask them to prepare a song-and-dance routine to put on for your guests before the disco starts. Supply the kids with goodie bags when they sit down to dinner to keep them quiet.

◆ Think about having a song written especially for you: my sister-in-law asked the crooner in her favourite Italian restaurant to pen one for her and her husband on their wedding day, and everyone was an emotional mess (in a good way!) listening to it.

◆ Reflect your cultures in your choice of music: go for national themes and celebratory dances – learn the steps if you have to. The Scots won't have a wedding without a piper!

◆ Give a strict list of favoured songs to the DJ or the band, so they can prepare a perfect set list. Ask for recommendations from your friends. Music is such an important aspect of the day, you can't afford to take a risk. Check that your DJ is bringing his full regalia with him – you want mirror balls, rope lights, lasers, and so on. Or if you don't want this stuff, tell him.

◆ Suggest a dress code for performers if they aren't wearing set costumes. They may be singing their hearts out, but a band in dirty tracksuits won't look like Buck's Fizz, will they?

◆ If you love a laugh, hire a stand-up comedian to entertain your guests while they are eating their dinner – just make sure he or she isn't offensive. Go back to the past by hiring jesters, wenches, knights and jousters to entertain your friends and family during the reception, especially if you're having your wedding in an old fort or castle.

◆ Place actors among the guests for the arrival drinks, to make things go outrageously, get everyone talking ... and to add something different – be it a murder mystery or a touch of glamour.

◆ If you love opera and want a touch of class, hiring a solo tenor or soprano will be cheaper than hiring a whole band – and it will appeal to the golden oldies!

◆ If you can't afford current chart toppers, think back a few years and hire a celebrity pop group from your youth. They'll add instant fun and nostalgia – and it's something guests will remember the day by.

◆ If you're having a period theme – and especially if you're going all Jane Austen – hire a silhouette cutter to sit in a corner and capture your guests' beauty or, er, drunken gurning!

◆ Traditionally, guests should not leave before the bride and groom depart. If you plan on dancing the night away and downing champers until the wee hours of the morning, get the DJ to announce this early on so that guests know they can leave when they like.

Chapter Seven

Lights, camera ... action

HOORAH FOR TECHNOLOGY and the modern age! Capturing your wedding day no longer consists of a bit of flash, bang, wallop outside the church and little else. The single, stuffy portrait of old, when photographers were a rare expense and couples were less vain than us celebrity-obsessed lot has been replaced with a plethora of machines invented to capture every sight and sound. They'll be creating smelly-vision next!

How to choose the right photographer and videographer

1. Ask recently married friends who they hired and also ask to see their wedding pictures.

2. When you make a shortlist, ask to see the photographers'/videographers' work from the last year, not five years ago.

3. Beware of people who don't use proper terms and references, or who ask for all the money upfront.

4. Perhaps ask an expert friend to come to meetings with you.

5. Make sure the photographer and videographer are willing to accept instructions, that is, for you to give them a list of things you do and don't want.

Soft focus

Darling, you look stunning – so capture it. Everyone has the bog-standard throwing confetti/family line-ups/cutting the cake photos, so liven things up by daring to be different:

◆ What about hiring a reportage photographer to capture the whole wedding, from engagement party and hen night to the morning after the night before, when your dress is lying, stained and crumpled, on the floor? Every picture will be part of an ever-evolving story.

◆ Think about shooting the whole day in black and white, especially if you're getting married in the bleak midwinter, full of grey skies and pasty people. Black and white adds a film-star sophistication to the images.

◆ Contact your local newspaper or magazine (or go national if you have the cash) and ask if they can recommend any cool snappers. Wedding photographers can be a little cheesy and may lack imagination, whereas someone who normally shoots anything from celebrities to war-torn cities will be original and creative.

◆ Use polarisers, coloured lenses and different processing to make the prints visually exciting and different.

◆ Give the photographer a free rein to shoot everything digitally, and then adjust and enhance to a point of air-brushed perfection at the editing stage.

Extra ideas for extra-cool photos:

◆ Dig around your grandparents' and parents' picture collections. Find your favourite wedding portrait and ask your photographer to recreate it. If possible take a copy of it and give it to him prior to the wedding.

◆ If you've always loved a particular moment in a film, get your snapper to do a similar set-up. As long as it's romantic; tell your groom he's not allowed the light-sabre scene in Star Wars (unless you want it, too!)

◆ For some reason, the pictures are a disaster. You've got your eyes shut in all of them, your beloved seems to have trouble keeping his tongue in his mouth and the pair of you didn't realise you had confetti stuck in your hair. What do you do? You get dolled up again and re-shoot. Yes, it's fake, but no, it doesn't matter. It's much better to re-do the photos straightaway – while the dress still fits – than regret not having at least one picture to give your mum and dad for ever.

◆ Set up a photo booth and allow guests to take their own pictures. Leave props and costumes around so they can really express themselves (but make sure you get in a few of the shots, too).

◆ Cameras on the table can be a good idea, but to stop wastage appoint a photo monitor to go around all the tables at the end of the meal to gather them up and finish the film. Pick them up from the developers yourself – your well-meaning mother may be offended by the bottom shots that inevitably end up on these cameras.

TARA, 30

❝ Many photographers bugger off as soon as the bride and groom have cut the cake, but we paid extra to keep ours around all evening. We knew that our friends would be most comfortable and funny after they'd had a few drinks and hit the dance floor. The photographer was amazing. He used a star filter, which reacts with light to form rainbows and prisms on the image, so the pictures came out with my glinty-eyed mates spinning round against a Las Vegas-style backdrop. It was the perfect way to capture the 'sparkly, dazzling best-night-of-my-life', as it's now known in our house. ❞

Fantasy photos

Yes, yes – you'll be far too busy meeting and greeting your nearest and dearest to pose for too long, but these pictures will haunt you (and grace your parents' mantelpiece) for years to come, so it's important to smile for your snapper.

So how do you get uniquely wonderful images of yourself and your beloved? You may feel uncomfortable in front of the camera, posing à la JLo, but don't panic – this isn't uncommon. If you want your wedding image to be complimented for the foreseeable future, do the following:

1. Practise. Have a trial run with your snapper; better still, have a trial run at your wedding venue. You and your man can look around, pick the most picturesque locations, get used to your photographer and ask him his opinion about styles and poses.

2. Get used to your face. Look closely in the mirror. Give yourself a grin. Do you suit a subtle, wry smile like the Mona Lisa? Or are you a full-watt, Cheshire cat kind of girl? The whiter your teeth, the bigger your beam. Think about getting your teeth whitened. It's an added expense, but quick, easy and image enhancing.

3. If you're not too keen on some aspects of your being (be it a big bottom, birth mark or bingo wings), mention it to the photographer in advance. Let the professional 'work around your issues' like a visually talented Frasier.

4. A few days before, do a modelling shoot with a friend and a digital camera. Snap and delete until you find some poses and angles you're happy with – and remember them!

5. When the big day arrives, ask the joker in your pack to stand near the photographer and shout encouragement – and funny one-liners – at you and the groom so you look natural and happy. Keep the jokes clean in case Granny is standing behind you.

Strike a pose

Look model-perfect with ease, by using some basic tips that keep Kate Moss looking slim and stunning:

1. Relax! Enjoy being a star for the day.

2. Wear highlighting and shimmering make-up to accentuate and tone your best bits. Add glitter to your décolletage and shoulders for extra sparkle. Eyebrows and lashes can disappear in flashlight, so think about having them carefully dyed a shade darker in advance.

3. Don't stand with your shoulders square to the camera. Slim them by standing side on.

4. Stand up tall. Bad posture adds inches. Imagine you have a wire running through your body and pulled upwards.

5. Hold your stomach in – remember this and you'll instantly come down a dress size.

6. Put one foot in front of the other and lean on your back foot (while tilting your hips) to minimise curvy hips and thighs.

7. Don't clench your fists. Let them hang loosely at your side or rest gently on your hips.

8. Don't hide behind your bouquet. Keep it at waist level.

9. Add height – and a slimline image for photos – by wearing high heels and putting your hair up.

10. If you – or important people like your mother or future mother-in-law – are wearing a hat, ensure their face (and most importantly eyes) are not hidden and that the brim doesn't shadow the face. The hat should be no wider than your shoulders or you'll look like a drag queen.

And for your close up:

1. Ask the photographer to count you in 1, 2, 3, and blink on one – that will avoid those weird droppy-lidded shots when your eyes are half-closed.

2. Don't do a diva pout. It will look false and daft.

3. Whatever you do, don't lift your chin too high in a bid to get rid of a double chin – the shot will be up your nostrils. Instead, lengthen your neck and don't jut your chin out; hold it naturally.

4. Look at past pictures and decide which is your best side – or ask your hairdresser, they'll know. Then make sure you turn your better side to the camera.

5. Take closer portraits in the 'golden hour', the last hour of sunlight. It will give you a golden glow, rather than in the harsh, show-all light of midday.

6. Make sure exposed limbs and décolletage have a light covering of moisturiser for a delicate shine.

7. Enjoy it – wink, stick your tongue out, giggle, pull faces. However you feel inside, let it out!

> **NB Pass on the above tips to your groom and brides-maids.** You don't want them to ruin the pictures by gurning or having their eyes closed when you've spent the last few months being self-obsessed and vain!

Picture perfect

If your pictures turn out brilliantly, flaunt them. Your parents will adore them, and your children will admire them as they get older, fall in love and weddings start to mean something to them. Don't just stick them in an album. Think about using images as:

◆ Slide shows.

◆ Mugs and plates.

◆ Pillowcases and cushions.

◆ Mouse mats and screen savers.

◆ On the case of your wedding video.

◆ As thank-you cards for wedding gifts.

◆ Key rings and magnets.

◆ Jigsaws and place mats.

You could even commission an artist to do a painting from one.

Film stars

Many brides are anti-wedding videos, thinking them too tacky or intrusive. Think again. The day will pass all too quickly, in a wonderful (if chaotic) blur – and for many couples their video provides an important reminder of their vows and speeches, and a valuable insight into what their guests got up to. These mini-movies don't have to be dull. Here's how:

1. Hire a professional. Don't risk giving the camera to a well-meaning but inexperienced friend, especially if

they've had a drink. Get a quote from three different videographers and pick the best quote – and person – for you. Ask newlywed friends for phone numbers and book early. If you can't afford a professional, ask at least three friends to capture your day. This is for back-up, and of course choice – you can get someone to edit the best bits together.

2. Capture elements of all aspects of the day – don't record the whole line-up!

3. Talk to the camera. Give mini-interviews to capture what you were thinking.

4. Record a karaoke-style musical montage. Play a sound-track and sing along to it. Get your guests to sing lines and formation dance to the chorus; the Bee Gees/Steps classic, 'Tragedy' is a favourite.

5. Use fade-in, fade-out, polarisers, coloured lenses and fil-ters to add drama.

6. If the church won't let you film the ceremony – as they often don't – just record the sound, then ask your video-grapher to go back and film the church and the surround-ing area to overlay to your audio memories.

7. Use title cards to flag up important people and sections of the day, and the end.

8. Shoot it in black and white for an arty feel (and it's more flattering!)

9. Start the video with photos of you and the groom grow-ing up ... to be the people you are today, on your wedding day. Finish the whole video with wedding pic-tures of your parents' big event.

10. Ask a friend to do a jokey commentary, sports-pundit style. It'll brighten up the dull bits.

> **NB If your videographer misses something**, go back and do it again. Yes it's fake, but you're the only one who knows, and while you're all dressed up, you might as well. Be a star in your own movie and do as many takes as you need, dahling.

Light years ahead

When you're looking to create a certain mood, the easiest and most alluring method is to play with the lighting. With a flick of a switch you can change the room from romantic, to cool, to cosy. So lighten up, modern girls! Don't get stuck in a rut thinking, for example, that you can only have candle-light at a winter wedding. Sod it! If you want candles and you're getting married in July, get fluorescent ones that can hang in trees and get your ushers to light them at 10.00 p.m.

Glow and behold

Daylight is wonderful, so if the weather's good, take the reception outside. Light up your life naturally by serving drinks and canapés while the sun sets in the distance and the blue sky turns to pinky-purple. If you're lucky enough to be getting married in the country on a clear day, have the dancing under a canopy of stars and the moon. Just make sure the borders of the area are clearly lit – you don't want to lose guests in bushes (unless that's their romantic inten-tion, of course).

Chinese lanterns add a touch of the orient to any event. If outside, drape them between trees, preferably in different colours and distances. They shouldn't look too ordered, but more like they've been thrown on with little thought.

Fairy lights add twinkle and sweetness to any space. Get the sets that can flash and change colour for a disco, or the plain bright white variety for a classy quiet do. Chilli-pepper lights are great for long, hot summer days, and rope lights can give you a retro 1970s feel. Whichever you choose, make sure the DJ booth is heavily decorated. That will draw in the dancers. Nothing gets the crowd going like dimmed, exciting lighting. If it's harsh people will be too embarrassed to break loose on the floor.

Chandeliers offer a decadence unmatched by any other form of lighting. If it's an outside do, you can still have them – just hire someone to rig them carefully. For extra glamour, hang glass beads and strings of pearls between them. Crystal drops will catch the light and reflect rainbow colours. Use simple glass Christmas decorations to the same effect.

Candles are the cheapest and simplest ways to light up your do. Personalise large church candles, use jewel-coloured gel candles, or put tea lights in clear, frosted or lace-covered votive holders. Tea lights now come in every colour – even gold – so choose carefully. And go for a scented variety if you wish, but be careful it's not too overpowering, or it could start a bout of sneezing or moan-ing. Don't forget the long, colourful ones for outdoors – perfect for calm, balmy evenings. Hurricane lamps are great for windy days, and try citronella candles in the height of summer when insects are around. Paint pots or glasses with your names and the wedding date, and guests will take them home as a reminder. Always remember to place candles safely where they can't tip over, and make sure that they are not too close to fabrics or other materials that could catch fire. Also, be extra cautious when having candles if there are children at the wedding.

Throw extra light on to the dance floor with strobes and beams – and what about big plasma screens? Use them to show old home videos, or footage from the hen and stag nights, or even just make music video compilations to dance to (or to watch while sitting in the corner with a pint).

If you're holding the wedding in large grounds, where guests have to stagger home from across fields or find their room at 3.00 a.m. in the main hotel, how about handing out commemorative torches? Unusual and practical, how about that?

If carefully managed, flaming torches can look stunning placed along main entrances and walkways – outdoors of course. Ask your venue if this is allowed, and then hire someone to keep them going throughout the evening reception. If you're planning a wedding at a castle or fort, these are a must!

BETH, 26

❛ We made our own canopy of stars for our August wedding. It was a dry – yet cloudy – evening, but it didn't matter because my brothers had set up net lights, hooked over the trees and forming an amazing roof of light next to the BBQ area. They were the white lights that glow and fade intermittently and everyone commented on the effect ... and it only set back my brothers a few hundred pounds at their local DIY superstore. Result! ❜

Good guy, Guy Fawkes

Well surely the most glamorously, spectacularly stunning end to a wedding is fireworks. It means your day really will end with a big bang. If you can't afford much, just hand out sparklers to guests to wave as you leave for your honeymoon. If you want to go the whole hog, hire a pyrotechnics expert and set the display to music and themes – you could even tie in the colours of the fireworks to your wedding colours.

Exciting electronica

When it comes to gadgets and lighting *et al.*, never say never. If you fancy setting up a mini-cinema on the premises for the under-16s, do it. If you want to set up fruit machines and one-armed bandits in the foyer, why not?

I've heard of the most remarkable wedding where the bride's father secretly hired a whole fairground with a big wheel and dodgems for the guests. It made the wedding truly memorable.

Another fun idea is to get the videographer to film live footage of guests arriving, or in the line-up for immediate transmission, to liven up the boring bits. Get a confident friend to interview guests about you and your groom as they're waiting in line; a bit like Joan Rivers on the red carpet at the Oscars.

If you're worried about the speeches, allow the nervous to record their words of wisdom in advance and show them on big screens. Or a nervous speaker can take the pressure off by turning the speech into a slide show (just hire a projector) where they simply talk the audience through each image. They don't even have to face the crowd.

> ### So, what else can you do?
>
> Basically, the world is your oyster, when it comes to electronic stuff, so check out innovation magazines a few months beforehand and see how technology can benefit you. If things seem to pricey, look at alternatives, ask for discounts, beg and borrow – it's your wedding day for goodness sake, which will hopefully be a one-off event.

Communication conundrums

In the past, when guests couldn't make the day they used to send a telegram, which was read by the best man during the speeches. Now, life can be much more exciting. Instead of a telegram, guests can send faxes and emails, which are not only free – which means they can drone on for longer – but private, so they really can get emotional and sentimental, and draw funny pictures for you to keep.

If you're upset that some guests can't make it, be they abroad or in hospital, how about setting up a live weblink from the ceremony? They'll almost feel like they are there. At the very least, set up mobile phones at the front so that special people can hear you take your vows.

Secrets of Success

♦ Practise your royal wave and do facial exercises every day for four weeks before the wedding. Everyone will want to take nice, jolly pictures of you, so make them feel special by waving directly at them with a massive grin on your face. The practising will relieve arm and face ache.

◆ Keep a photo diary on a personal web address, so people can see your engagement ring, the venue, a map of how to get there. Store your pics on CD for easy editing and access.

◆ Ask your professional photographer to put his images on a website so that guests can choose the ones they want copies of without hassling you.

◆ Make sure someone on the top table has a camera to capture those intimate, special moments.

◆ Newlyweds can email a digital picture of themselves, with a thank-you note, to all their guests while still on honeymoon! Another fun, pictorial idea for thank-you notes is to use a beautiful image of the church, or your bouquet, or the back of the wedding car as you're driving away with 'Just Married' on the bumper.

◆ Look into installing an illuminated dance floor and your guests will hit the floor and throw some shapes. The squares, which light up when you step on them, really excite boogiers! Invest in some electronic dance mats. They're cheap and easy – and your guests can take it in turns to practise their moves by following the lit-up arrows. Get a few, put them in a line, and your guests will be able to formation dance without even trying.

◆ Escape wedding hell a few weeks before your big day by going to a pop concert. Not only will you forget all your worries but also you can purchase a selection of lights, shakers and deely-boppers. Hand them out to guests once the disco starts – the luminous necklaces and bracelets are particularly effective (if a little 1980s). Glow sticks are also good, and available from most big nightclubs.

◆ If you're holding your wedding outside, try changing the colours of the buildings and trees in the vicinity between courses. It's cheap and easy to do – but very dramatic. I've seen five-star hotels do this and it never fails to wow. When actress Alyson Hannigan got hitched in California, childhood pictures of the couple were projected on to fabric stretched between palm trees.

◆ If you want young pageboys and flower girls but you're not sure they'd love to walk up the aisle with you, make it fun. Get a mini-version of your wedding car and get the older attendants to pull them. Ask a trusty friend to add a little 'Just Married' sign after the ceremony for the pictures.

◆ For outdoor atmosphere, dot glow cubes around for seating and get your names made in tube lettering to hang over the entrances.

◆ Sort out a microphone and a spotlight for the speech-makers. Speeches are even more long and boring when you're stuck at the back and can't hear a word.

◆ If you're very cool and think even fireworks are passé, look into running a laser show – there's less chance of people getting burnt or kids getting scared, too.

◆ Are there a few children and teenagers at the wedding whom you want to keep quiet? Put them on a table together with a couple of Gameboys. They won't make a sound.

◆ The old ones are the best: when it's time for the last, slow dance of the evening, make sure the DJ dims the lights as a signal to guests that it's time to go.

Chapter Eight

The last word in style

NEVER UNDERESTIMATE THE POWER of the written word – or a printed one for that matter. And the spoken word is very important too! Think of invitations as the wedding's opening act – the clue to all the glory and drama to come – then follow up with beautifully designed stationery at the reception. And don't forget that the best speeches and readings will ring in your ears for years to come!

Post it

Before the first guest takes a seat at the ceremony, you can set the right impression for your big day by sending out perfect invitations. Use these to give clues to colour schemes, themes, surprises and the general mood. Send out invites three months beforehand, ask for details of any special requirements and include RSVP cards and envelopes for your guest's convenience.

Some inviting ideas are:

◆ For a summer wedding, send invites on fans that the guests can then bring to cool themselves down.

◆ Get a coat-of-arms expert to design you and your betrothed's family crest and use the colours as a base for the invites. Very Posh 'n' Becks.

◆ Go for grown-up glamour. Black script on gold-edged white card is timelessly elegant, and will decorate anyone's mantelpiece.

◆ Print the invitation on to personalised balloons – the party starts immediately!

◆ Wrap the invitation in the same fabric as the bridesmaids' dresses and attach it with crystals and sequins.

◆ If you're feeling handy, cross-stitch or embroider your invitations, or at least your guests' names – how rewardingly *Little Women*.

◆ Design an invitation using your parents' wedding photo, and, of course your new in-laws' portrait, too. It will add retro glamour and please your parents, But perhaps not if they are now divorced. Alternatively, how about using childhood photos of you two: the bride and groom?

◆ It's terribly modern, but how about emailing everyone a mystery website address. They'll log on, get the invite and the details, and you could do a countdown calendar and a diary building up to the big day. Keep it going afterwards to add your photos, guests' messages and your list of presents (everyone will want to know what you got!)

◆ Send a professional photographer or artist to the church or venue and use their most stunning image as the invitation.

◆ Go Olde English: use a rolled scroll of parchment, write your message with black ink (quill optional) and seal with red wax. If a friend can do calligraphy, bribe him or her to write them for you. You'll owe many drinks, remember.

NB Add a little extra to the invites. When we posted ours, we stuffed the envelopes full of gold stars – which we then replicated on the tables at the reception. Many friends said what a pleasant surprise it was – although it took a while to pick them off the carpet! So think about adding confetti, sweets, photos, maps, song sheets ... in fact anything to add interest.

Sealed with a kiss

The invite inside the envelope may be stunning, but if the thing that pops through the letterbox is dull, who cares? Jazz it up by using glitter spray, gluing on sequins, attaching feathers, sealing it with a personalised red wax stamp, using commemorative stamps, writing messages on the back, or making the envelope something really special. My recently married friends sent out their invitations in silver tubes, and the invite was rolled inside it. It caused a nightmare for the postman but I'd never seen anything like it! Whatever the score, always make sure the envelope is in your wedding colours, or in a matching shade to the invite inside – anything else will look wrong.

SASHA, 35

❝ We got married in a ski resort in Austria, so I got an old ski poster and recreated it on a Mac to include our names and details of the wedding as the invitation. Our wedding march song was 'Happy Heart' by Andy Williams. We didn't have hymns, but for the bidding prayers we asked three friends to make something up just for us. It was so touching and lovely. At the reception, we had toasts between each course from different people – short and sweet, then just the best man's speech, so it didn't drag on. On everyone's places we left an envelope with a personal note inside to each person saying what they meant to us as a friend. That went down very well! ❞

Cutting costs

Invites are expensive, so use your imagination. You could:

♦ Send an email card, just get confirmation that all have been sent!

♦ Get a favourite photo of you and your betrothed multi-printed, and place a sticker on the back of each with all details.

- Buy blank cards, or wedding invites from your local stationers and make them a little more exciting by including some penny sweets or sequins.

- Ask a creative friend to get busy on their computer and design and print something just for you.

- Use plain card but write details in fountain pen for an expensive finish.

- Send hand-written letters asking for guests' attendance, rather than sending universal invites. This will be warmly received and make the guests feel special.

- If you're having a small wedding, just invite people over the phone and make sure they put it in their diaries. Friends and family will appreciate a call to hear your good news, so this will eliminate an invite anyway.

Perfect paper

Now your invitations have set the tone, carry on the originality by getting other wedding stationery personalised – and beautiful. Don't just panic and rush out any old orders of service, tie them in to the theme and make them memorable. There's a lot to think about:

- Reply cards.

- Meal instruction cards.

- Orders of service.

- Place cards.

- Place mats.

- Menu cards.

- Table name/number markers.

- Table plan.

- Signs for directions between rooms.

- Dance/song request slips.

- Bar menus.

- Cocktail lists.

- The speeches (printed for guests to take home).

- Cake boxes.

- Thank-you cards.

If you can plan your stationery requirements in advance, it will save a lot of stress, and you'll save a fair bit of money. Although stationery sounds like a dull thing to plan it can be fun. For example, if you don't like the signs on the toilets at your reception venue, get personalised ones made and put up – a picture of you for the ladies, and your groom for the gents.

My husband and I had matchboxes printed with our names and wedding date on and left them on the bar and in the toilets. We also had personalised favour boxes made in the same colours and textures as our invitations. So that the dance floor would be full at all times, we printed DJ request slips (with pictures of us with our favourite pop stars on) and put them on each table, so guests could get their favourite songs played and dedicated to them.

FLAVIA, 32

❝ While I was in the stationer's checking my invites and orders of service, I spotted another printing service they did with apparently growing success. You can now get diamanté-studded messages printed on to clothing, and it looks fab. I treated myself to a bikini with 'Mrs Rushmore' in sequins across the bottom for my honeymoon. It was a great success! ❞

Wedding readings

Now, I am a sucker for the classics, so risked being quite unoriginal with my wedding readings – but I absolutely love Shakespeare's 'Love Alters Not' sonnet and the bible's Corinthians 13, and I knew they would mean a lot to the people we asked to read them.

The most important things when choosing a reading are:

1. To think about who is reading it. Will they be nervous and need something short, or do they have a striking, booming voice that will keep everyone mesmerised for a good few minutes?

2. Are you religious? Think about your own views, and find out what is allowed in your chosen venue.

3. Pick something that means something to you – even if (God forbid!) it's the lyrics to 'Lovin' You' by Minnie Ripperton!

4. Don't do it in a foreign language. The majority of your guests will be mystified ... and not in a good way.

5. Have a laugh. Just because it's a wedding reading it does-n't have to be serious.

If you're at a loss, but you know you want something different yet still beautifully written and romantic, here is an unbeatable list of some unusual and appropriate prose:

'A Love Song', Theodosia Garrison

'A Magic Moment I Remember', Pushkin

'A Wedding-Song', John White Chadwick

'Air and Angels', John Donne

'Always for the First Time', Andre Breton

'At Last', Elizabeth Akers Allen

'Attraction', Ella Wheeler Wilcox

'Bright Star, Would I Were Steadfast as Thou Art',
John Keats

'Come Slowly', Emily Dickinson

'Destiny', Edwin Arnold

'First Love', John Clare

'For Each Ecstatic Instant', Emily Dickinson

'Friendship after Love', Ella Wheeler Wilcox

'I Would Live in Your Love', Sara Teasdale

'If I Were Her Lover', Madison Julius Cawein

'In My Sky at Twilight', Pablo Neruda

'Is Love, then, so Simple', Irene Rutherford Mcleod

'Joy', Sara Teasdale

'Life in a Love', Robert Browning

'Love and Friendship', Emily Brontë

'Love is Enough', William Morris

'Love's Philosophy', Percy Bysshe Shelley

'Lullaby', W. H. Auden

'Marriage Morning', Alfred, Lord Tennyson

'My First Love', F. Scott Fitzgerald

'The First Day', Christina Rossetti

'The Perfect Woman', William Wordsworth

'Young and Old', Charles Kingsley

And some of you lucky brides will be able to choose a great work, personalised for you. Ask the groom, or your father to read one of the following if you're named so:

'Annabel Lee', Edgar Allen Poe

'Annie Laurie', William Douglas

'Go Lovely Rose', Edmund Waller

'Jenny Kissed Me', Leigh Hunt

'Love Song For Alex', Margaret Walker

'Ruth', Thomas Hood

'To Anthea III', Robert Herrick

'To Celia', Ben Johnson

'To Jane', Percy Bysshe Shelley

'To Mary', John Clare

'Upon Julia's Clothes', Robert Herrick

Do your own thing

Dare you ask a friend to freestyle on the biggest day of your life, with all your mates and family present? Of course you should – if you have a friend willing and able enough to take on the challenge. Remember: standing up and delivering a speech or reading is terrifying stuff (my chief bridesmaid did a speech at my wedding and had to take beta-blockers to calm her nerves!). And do you have a friend that could sit down with a blank piece of paper and come up with something witty or moving? If you do, make the most of them. A friend gave a hilarious reading in the church for my husband and I – and it even made the rather stern vicar giggle.

A few months ago, I was asked to write something for a friend's wedding. Sitting down with pen and paper is daunting, but if you've asked someone to do the same for you, leave this page open in front of them for a few hints:

1. Don't be offensive; it won't be suitable for a ceremony, so no swearing or prejudice.

2. Talk about both the bride and groom – she may be your friend, but it's their wedding day.

3. Ask around. Call and email close friends and family: what makes them think of the couple?

4. Flick through photo albums to remind you of the good times.

5. Lightly ridicule their flaws, and flatter their egos.

6. No one expects Lord Byron. As long as it loosely rhymes and is read clearly and loudly, the congregation will love it (anything's better than sitting through a ten-minute-long sanctimonious recital).

Other ideas for readings

◆ Investigate your CD collection or iPod. If you first danced together to a U2 song, or your favourite film has a great soundtrack, recite those words. My husband read a verse and chorus from the *Moulin Rouge* movie at a recent wedding, and the slow look of realisation on the bride and groom's face was priceless.

◆ Are you creative types who may have written love poems to each other during your courtship? Ask a trusted friend to read the best one aloud during the service.

◆ Be surprised – lose control of something. Get a good mate to take over, and get them to deal directly with the minister or registrar to make sure it's appropriate.

◆ Ask someone to give a brief history on marriage in the country in which you're tying the knot, or a brief history of your courtship and how everyone got here today.

◆ Create a recipe with your designated reader, and ask them to read it how a chef would do. For example, 'A bride and groom, 25 years old, lightly salted with tears. Three sweet flower girls, doused in lavender. Four Spanish señoritas, in fresh from Barcelona', and so on.

I PROMISE TO ENTERTAIN

If you're getting married in a church, synagogue, temple or mosque, you don't have any choice about what to say in your vows. If you're getting married in a registered location, you do. Jennifer Aniston and Brad Pitt were toe-curlingly sweet when they exchanged their vows, promising to make banana smoothies and massage feet, which may go down OK in La-La Land, Los Angeles, but will have your great-aunt sniggering in the second row. If you are writing your own vows, make them sincere, heartfelt and romantic, but avoid schmaltz. And don't be overly sexual. I have heard a bride utter the stomach-churning words, 'I will give myself to you sexually whenever you desire me', and it didn't go down too well.

Stunning speeches

The speeches are both the most eagerly awaited, and dreaded, part of the wedding day. The guests are seated and lubricated by a few glasses of vino, willing the speakers to make them laugh, cry, sigh … and be outraged with mock indignation. This puts a lot of pressure on the top table to be as entertaining as possible.

> **LAURA, 29**
>
> ❝ I heard the loveliest speech at a recent wedding – and it was the groom who delivered it. It can be a side effect of getting hitched that the couple become very self-absorbed and egocentric, but this couple couldn't have been more different. The groom started by saying, 'This year isn't only a special year for us, but lots of other people who mean a lot to us ...', and he then proceeded to warmly congratulate the other couples who had tied the knot that year, the women who were pregnant or had just had a child, the older couples who were celebrating landmark anniversaries and the lovebirds who had just announced their engagements. There was lots of clapping and cheering – and crying of course – and a real feeling of 'Wow, what a good bloke!' ❞

A new, modern idea is for the bride to say a few words – but I would offer a few words of warning. Brides can work themselves up into a hormonal frenzy in the weeks before their wedding. Putting that extra pressure on yourself to stand in front of a crowd and be witty and charming (when inside, you're a Bridezilla with tear-duct issues!) could be tricky. Why not just jot down a few notes, and give them to your mum? Then if the mood takes you, feel free to freestyle.

The same should be said for asking your bridesmaids to say a few words. I still feel so guilty about innocently asking my mate to stand up and say a few words. Your bridesmaids' main responsibility is to look after you – and how can they do that when they're practising their lines in the mirror?

If you or your friends want to speak, therefore, think

long and hard about the extra stress you're putting on yourselves – and if it's worth it.

Saying all this, the poor men don't have an option about it – they must do some kind of address, even if it's a quick toast and a thank you.

Forget tradition, if you must, and make it easier by:

◆ Getting the speeches out of the way during the welcome drinks, or before the starter is served at mealtime.

◆ Setting a time limit of, say, three minutes per speaker.

◆ Handing out set jokes (all the winners) that they could include on the day to the best man and father of the bride while they are preparing their speeches.

◆ Using visual aids: if you're too nervous to talk, pre-record a mini-film about your partner, the wedding, your guests, and so on. Or shift the attention away from your blushing cheeks, by asking the ushers to hand out hilarious photographs.

NB The best man's barrage! As the bride, you will not receive any information on what the best man is going to say – and quite right, too. Whatever he does say is in jest, and out of fondness for his great mate; it has very little to do with you. So don't overreact, get hurt or tell him off. It's lads being lads. I've seen a bride slap a best man, and it was unique – but it wasn't pretty!

Joking apart

It's not easy to be funny, but here are the classics:

◆ This wedding has been so emotional that even the cake is in tiers (the best man).

◆ The week before the wedding, a robber stole my credit card. I haven't reported it to the police because he spends less than my new wife (the groom).

◆ My daughter was worried she'd mess up the service, so I said just remember: you walk up the aisle, stand at the altar and sing the first hymn. Imagine the groom's face when she walked towards him, mouthing 'aisle-altar-hymn' (father of the bride).

◆ I can't speak for long because of my throat (said in croaky voice). If I say too much the groom has threatened to cut it (best man).

◆ I've been told to keep this short, like so many things in the groom's life (best man).

◆ Being asked to be best man is rather like being asked to sleep with the Queen. It's a great honour but you wish someone else would do it (best man).

Top toasts

It is a formal requirement to thank the wedding party, but if a friend has been there just for you during a stressful few months – get a round of applause for them too! Instead of simply saying 'Thanks to –', do it in rhyme, or sing it!

And when you're handing out thank-you presents, you don't have to stick to the usual bouquet of flowers for the mothers and bottle of whisky for the dads. Have more fun than that. Book them a weekend away while you're away relaxing on your honeymoon. Or buy them a special photo frame or album – they'll be so proud of all your wedding photos they'll want to store them properly. Don't feel you have to get your bridesmaids something traditional and formal. They'll never wear a brooch! If they're all mad for Birkenstock sandals – get them each a pair in a different colour.

Go customise crazy with everyone else: get them commemorative champagne glasses, T-shirts or a bottle of wine with the date of your wedding on, so they'll always remember they played a special part in your special day.

Telegrams should be read out – but only if the writers aren't present. And keep it brief (read the full transcript when you've got more time) and think about adding interest by getting a sweepstake going around the tables on how long it will take to complete all the speeches and toasts – this keeps the men listening!

Secrets of Success

♦ Send your invitations from somewhere interesting, so that they get a memorable postmark – be it the city where you and your groom met at university, or from the country where he proposed, or even a postal district with a romantic name.

♦ Add quotes from your favourite film or poem to the invitation for a personal touch, and ask a friend with nice handwriting to write them for you (reward them fairly with flowers and chocolates – this is a gruelling task!).

♦ Phone close friends who have RSVPed 'plus one' to ask their guest's name – it'll make their friend feel welcome and will look less bizarre on the table plan.

◆ Keep the list of addresses you have got together for your wedding invites – this will prove invaluable for thank-you cards and at Christmas.

◆ Receiving an invitation to a wedding two months after everyone else is a sure sign you're on the B-list. Minimise embarrassment by sending out all the invites a little later, and demanding RSVPs within two weeks (to speed it up, allow people to reply by email or text).

◆ Keep your guests well informed about the day ahead. Print up a timetable and leave it next to the table plan or at the bar, with times for toasts, dinner and other key items, such as the last dance and carriages.

◆ Get inspired by your favourite artists. Interpret the wonder of Monet, Degas or Turner into your colourful, original own designs.

◆ If you have young nieces and nephews, how about getting them to paint pictures of how they think you'll look on your wedding day, and use that image on invitations, orders of service and menu cards? It may not be flattering, but it will be very funny!

◆ Your wedding invitation and evening reception invite do not need to be the same. For a more informal and fun idea, send the party guests their instructions on card shaped like a bottle of champers or a martini glass.

◆ Don't print up menu cards and orders of service for everyone – save time and money by supplying one between two. This means that all the women get to take them away as a souvenir.

◆ If you would love a friend to give a speech, but they are more talented musically – ask the supervisor if they can sing or play a message to you rather than do a formal reading.

◆ At the evening buffet, print up mini-flags to stick into the various canapés to indicate what's in them – in your wedding colours, of course.

◆ Think about getting beer mats printed with your photo on for the bar and tables. And at the same time, print badges for the bar staff to wear, too.

◆ In the evening, hand around a special notebook to allow your guests to leave their personal messages and signatures.

◆ For some unusual printing, think about getting a secret tattoo (non-permanent) of your new husband's name and your wedding date to reveal on your honeymoon.

◆ Frame your table plan. My husband and I hung ours in our dining room, and when our wedding guests came round for a meal after the celebration they would always search out their names between courses.

◆ Remember to place an announcement in your local paper, or a favourite magazine – this is a very old-fashioned, forgotten part of a wedding but something that I declare should be brought back! What a lovely souvenir!

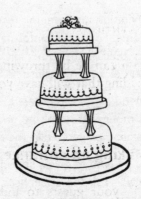

Chapter Nine

Sprinkle some sparkle

HOW UNCONVENTIONAL ARE YOU and your new husband? Very! Show the world just how fun and fabulous you can be by throwing in a few magic touches to your wedding that will have your guests talking for days. Shine on!

Making an entrance

Forget about asking your guests to indulge in a warm glass of Buck's Fizz and making their way limply through a line-up to take a seat at a plain-Jane table. You can do better than that. When your guests first arrive at the reception they should be dazzled by the decoration and the ambience. How about welcoming guests in an unusual manner? Human sculptures, dancers, Venetian masked men, spacemen holding trays of cocktails. Go mad. It will shock everyone – and let them know this is a one-of-a-kind wedding. If this seems a little too full-on, even waiters in penguin suits offering champagne will set the style. This is the time to start the sparkle.

◆ Throw a welcoming cocktail party, using celebrity look-alikes. Have an Elton John wannabe on the piano in the corner. Ask the Queen to greet your foreign guests. Charlie Chaplin and Marilyn Monroe can serve drinks.

◆ As guests walk in, ask cloakroom attendants to take coats and bags, and hand out themed tickets in your wedding colours, or with pictures of you on them. Leave sweets and matchboxes on the counter.

◆ Set up a picture area, so that all arriving guests feel like stars when they have their photograph taken. Why not lay out a red carpet, so that people feel like they're attending a super-cool event? Hire a doorman to remove the velvet rope when he's checked off the guest on his list. After all, you're only having VIPs at your wedding.

◆ If there is a corridor or waiting area, decorate the walls with pictures from the hen and stag nights, recent weddings of friends and families, or you and your groom as children.

◆ Make a 'love tunnel', like a cheesy 1950s American college ball, out of red and pink helium balloons for guests to walk through.

◆ Spray some scent. Smell is a powerful – but overlooked – sense. Mimic the fragrance of your bouquet, or if you're about to go off on a tropical honeymoon, the smell of tropical fruits and flowers.

◆ If you're having a line-up, don't let it drag out by asking the world and his mother to stand with you. Keep it to the couple and their parents – and play music loudly so that you can't be stuck in repetitive and time-consuming conversations.

◆ Once guests are seated, the dining entertainment should start. Ask the band to strike up or the DJ to start mixing as soon as the first few people are at their table.

Delicious decor

Although most of the focus at a wedding will be on the bride and groom, don't forget about everywhere else. You can look stunning, and the food can be amazing, but if you're holding the reception in a drab community centre, your guests will remember.

◆ Cover up any ugly signs imaginatively. Use netting, silk and satin to disguise ugly corners. Brighten up dull corridors with balloons, photos, artwork and lights. A simple string of fairy lights can turn an unused broom cupboard into a magical cloakroom.

◆ Don't worry about being tacky or OTT. If you want to cover every wall with projected images of your childhood, do it. It's better to do too much than too little – especially where weddings are concerned.

◆ The old-fashioned banner has been in the wedding wasteland for too long. Bring it back with some sparkle, and hang banners above doors and windows with your names, pictures and the date on. These are cheap but very cheerful.

◆ Flowers are expensive, so fill up on greenery, grass and dried flora. Spray with glitter for instant effect.

◆ Trim jam jars and pots with ribbon and use as night-lights. Cover every available surface for a dazzling effect.

◆ If your service and reception are being held in different places, save money on decor by instructing your ushers to bring the flowers from the service with them to liven up the next venue.

◆ Ask a local artist to produce work to your set theme and hang it carefully in a well-lit position. Try to get a good deal by saying you'll attempt to flog it for them while it's on display. You never know, your guests may fall in love with the work.

◆ Hire fake trees, plastic flowers and transportable ornamental ponds for instantly outrageous decor. You could even ask a water specialist to set up a water-fall for real wow factor.

◆ Garlands aren't just for Christmas. String tinsel and flowers between beams and windows all year round. Attach with ribbons in your wedding colours.

◆ Visit your local theatre company or drama group and ask to borrow their more flamboyant backdrops for a show-stopping room.

TOILET HUMOUR

You don't want your wedding reception to be marvellous only for guests to have to spend a fair time queuing in a dark and dingy lavatory. Pay attention to the loos when the reception manager is giving you a tour of the venue. They should be near the bar and where you will be eating. Ideally they should be yours exclusively, and plentiful enough for the crowd you're expecting.

Think about brightening up the loos (women do tend to gossip in them, and it will certainly take you ages to go to the loo wearing a big dress, so you'll want to make them cosy) with nice towels, scented soaps and hand lotions. Maybe even sprinkle some sweet-smelling soap petals in pretty boxes around the hand basins. These are available from large chemists and department stores. Fresh flowers and a selection of perfume will impress everyone! Perhaps even leave a goodie-box of chewing gum and breath fresheners, like you will find in the VIP rooms of swish nightclubs.

Table talk

Your guests will spend a good few hours at their designated table – for the meal and the speeches, and for keeping their handbags and pints of lager safe once the disco starts. So make them memorable by calling them something other than 1, 2, 3 or A, B, C.

ROSE, 29

6 Instead of numbers, we're naming our tables after our favourite love songs. The top table will be the song that we will then have for our first dance, and another table, headed up by one of the bridesmaids, will be called after my song for Lee; his ushers will be on a table named after his song for me. One of my business clients did this at their wedding a few years ago and I'd always remembered it. To personalise our day, we're going to have a picture of the artist and the chorus of the song on a stand in the middle of each table. The good thing about this is that there is no hierarchy; guests won't feel bad if they are seated at table number 20, for example. Also, we're going to pick who goes on which table and with which song carefully; for example, Lee's family will love to be seated at Ella Fitzgerald's 'At Last' table. 9

Why not name your tables after something special? Here are a few suggestions:

◆ Your favourite number-one hits from the 1980s, 1990s, 2000s or last year, then play them at the disco later and ask each table to hit the floor when their table's song is played.

◆ Historical references – your schools, first pets, mums' names, and so on.

◆ Give the group on each table a name, such as 'The Crazy Gang', for example.

◆ Instead of a simple, Table 1 or Table 2, write the plan using Roman numerals or the Greek alphabet.

- Colours, and decorate the table in the same hue.

- Your favourite sweets, and then leave the relevant sweet on each place setting.

- Different periods in history, and use a candle or decorative feature to reflect those years.

- Your favourite cities.

- Your favourite actors, singers or writers.

- Key locations of your courtship.

- Key people who can't be with your today, such as grandparents, friends, and so on.

- The first ten songs you will play at the disco that evening.

- The flowers in your bouquet.

> **NB If you have over 200 guests**, it's best simply to number the tables and alphabetise the names on the table plan. If you have fewer guests, and finding the correct table won't be so confusing, have some fun.

Make a fable from your table

These days there is no excuse for a boring table. Guests arrive at a wedding expecting to see some colour, flair and even a few little take-home gifts.

At my own wedding – aware that my dad, the groom and his best man are all talkers – I needed to add a lot of special gift ideas to keep everyone seated and contented. First of all, we put pots of bubbles on every table that had children so that they could happily blow themselves away and leave their parents to have a good time. Then we laid out pictures of the groom as a baby to illustrate the best man's speech.

Here are some ideas for affordable – and accessible – products you can find on the Internet or via a good wedding planner:

◆ Guests' names can be written on leaves, photos, pebbles, shells, feathers, fabric – don't stick to folded card. Make paper boats or butterflies for names to be written on. Laminate name tags, or personalise badges for guests to wear.

◆ Gifts can be put in boxes with bows and tags, and come in different shapes (animals, men's dinner jackets, top hats or small bags can be made of card or sheer fabric), so don't settle for dull wrapping.

◆ Fill large Perspex boxes with jelly babies, flying saucers, chocolate eggs, cola cubes, sugared almonds – whatever confectionery suits your colour scheme

◆ Party poppers and bubbles will add a dramatic finish to the speeches and should be laid out on the table. Streamers and Flutter Flickers are also good.

◆ Cameras can be fun – but don't expect good results. Attach tags or stickers saying 'Please use me up!'

◆ Napkins can be personalised: print your initials, family crest, or picture on them.

◆ An aquarium makes a stunning table decoration. Fill with pebbles and shells in your wedding colour.

◆ Sprinkle glitter or confetti over the table. Visit good stationers to find 'Just Married' or 'Congratulations'. It's also worth trying to get your names made into confetti. If not, stars, cherubs, flowers and hearts are always good – as long as they're in your colours! Crystals, sequins, shells and freeze-dried petals can also be sprinkled for effect.

♦ Tubes of chocolate truffles, Smarties or sherbets are unusual and double as take-home gifts. Lovehearts stating 'Just Married' are winners.

♦ Mini-sparklers can be left on placemats for dessert time – and they come in heart and star shapes as well as the traditional sticks. Or see if you can get them made to order formed into your initials.

♦ Put menu cards in photo frames that guests can take home with them.

♦ Leave personalised miniatures on the table: Bailey's, Archer's or Bacardi for the girls, whisky, tequila or brandy for the boys.

♦ Keep the kids occupied with drawing sets, balloons, hats, bubbles, Lego or teddy bears.

♦ Why keep crackers for Christmas? Pearlised crackers in non-Christmassy colours are great all year round.

♦ Leave boxes of table trivia out for the guests to answer between courses.

♦ Personalised lollies and sticks of rock can be kept or eaten.

♦ Get ornate place markers or table-number holders. Hearts, angels and mini-Bride 'n' Grooms are good fun.

♦ For cheap and cheerful colour, tie balloons to the centre of each table. Go for helium heart-shaped, pearlised, metallic or personalised versions. Keep them secure with special wedding weights, shaped like top hats or champagne bottles.

Sitting pretty

Decorate the chairs with ribbon, sheer fabric, flowers and greenery. Ask your florist to design something unique to you. If flowers are too expensive, simply drape each chair in ribbon or ask permission to spray them with glitter or paint in the colour of your wedding. You can buy speciality ribbon with your names and the date of your wedding printed on.

Tablecloths can be as classic (crisp, white linen) or as amazing (try metallic for the ultimate in light and sparkle) as you wish. Just make sure each guest has the correct, clean cutlery for the meal you're providing and enough space to eat without banging elbows.

Leave gifts and cards on the place mats for guests celebrating a birthday or special event that week. This will make them feel special.

KEELEY, 25

6 In the centre of each table at my wedding there was a vase filled with marshmallows and candy canes and a candle-lit chocolate fondue. I had all the menus printed on to chocolate slabs with the same picture we used on our invites: a school picture of Chris and I from our first year at school when we were five. Strangely enough we were sitting next to each other and he is even looking at me! We also had this picture made into stamps for the invitation envelopes. The wording said 'Sweet Hearts' to tie in with our sweets theme. 9

> **HAYLEY, 30**
>
> ❝ We tried to make our tables a little different for our reception by having pictures of our guests' faces imposed on caricatures at each place setting. We opted for pictures where the guest was pulling a funny face or one that had been taken years earlier, so it would provide amusement around the table. We also decided to go for lottery tickets as favours instead of the more traditional bag of sugared almonds. We thought the guests would be more appreciative if they won! We also left paper and pens on each seat and encouraged everyone to guess how long the best man's speech would last for. The person closest to the correct time won a prize. ❞

Dream themes

If you and your partner really love something, and all your friends associate you with it, why not try a theme: if you are two football season-ticket holders, a football lover's wedding won't be a nasty shock for your guests. Neither would an Olde England theme if you're history graduates getting married in a castle. Just give your guests plenty of warning if you want them to dress up, and don't go mad if they're too embarrassed or harassed to join in – fancy dress and acting up isn't everyone's cup of tea. Just make sure you're comfortable. A British couple recently tied the knot dressed as Marge and Homer Simpson, which made them both happy (and provided their 15 minutes of fame), but they were wise enough not to insist that the congregation dressed as other residents of Springfield!

Themes to think about include:

◆ Eastern promise, for jewels and vibrant colours, spicy food and lanterns.

◆ Fairy tale, for cupids, angels and all things sweet and delicate.

◆ Colour, ask all guests to come in a certain shade, and serve food and drinks in the same palette.

◆ Tea time, act refined while serving cucumber sandwiches and Earl Grey.

◆ Honeymoon heaven, replicate where you're escaping to.

◆ Film fantasy, if you've always wanted to be Danny and Sandy, now's your chance.

◆ Pick a decade, and tie in the decor, your dress and the drinks to it.

◆ Swan Lake, lots of white and feathers, and stirring classical music.

◆ Minimalist; for the ultimate modern couple simple chic is everything.

◆ Summer holiday, for bright colours, umbrellas in cocktails and waiters in Hawaiian shirts.

KIM, 27

❝ I have loosely based my wedding on musicals. The bridesmaids are dressed as something from *Moulin Rouge*, wearing long black fishtailed skirts, and red-and-cream whalebone bodices, with red-and-cream silk flower corsages and matching hairpieces. Instead of flowers they are holding

red-and-black marabou fans with ribbons attached. I had
these made by a clothes designer whose outfits I adore and
who 'doesn't make bridal wear' (in her words – however, in
this case she changed her mind! Don't be afraid to ask). The
theme for the decorations comes from *Chitty Chitty Bang
Bang*, so everything is sweets and ribbons, and I have
ordered the score of the show for the band to play. After
the wedding breakfast, morris dancers will entertain. I love
watching them and thought it would be nice for the foreign
visitors we have coming to see something traditionally
English. ❜

Good day sunshine!

In good weather, the wedding world is your oyster. Add
unique touches by:

◆ Hiring formation flyers to sweep across your horizon –
hell, you can even get them to draw a heart in the sky!

◆ Setting up a donkey derby for the children to have rides.

◆ Getting a village fête atmosphere by having a coconut
shy, cake stand and lots of brightly coloured bunting.

◆ Hiring a bouncy castle and adventure playground.

◆ Telling guests they are allowed to bring their pets with
them for an instant mini-zoo.

◆ Setting up a maypole for drunken dancing, and a band-
stand for outdoor entertainment.

◆ Supplying deckchairs and sun-loungers for guests to chill
out on.

◆ Providing fans for the girls and water pistols for the boys.

◆ Hiring a yacht or steamer and serving the pre-dinner drinks on board.

◆ Releasing a pair of doves into the sky as a symbol of your love.

> **NB If the weather is disappointing**, boss the ushers into setting up more seating indoors, and bring in whatever decorations can be saved. If you've had a few days' notice of an unpredicted downpour, think about setting up some entertainment inside – be it a cinema screen or even asking to have the log fires lit.

Crazy, crazy nights

This really is your night to feel special – so if you've always wanted to hold a limbo competition or try fire eating, now is your time to do it. No one can refuse a bride anything – and they even have to cheer and clap while she does it!

Our wedding went on way past the set time of midnight, and the DJ was forced to carry on playing tunes until 1.00 a.m. The reason? Well, our friends and family are wonderful, energetic people but I really do put it down to the idea I had to give everyone a party pack as the disco started. The waiting staff walked round with these surprise bags after the dinner and everyone went crazy. Suddenly the room was buzzing and colourful, at a time when people normally start flagging and looking at their watches. Tambourines, maracas, hats, flowers, blowers, streamers ... the guests had a great time and the photographs are fantastic – and they only cost a few pounds per person. The money we saved on hiring the men's suits and my tiara instead of buying them easily covered the costs. It was worth every penny.

Other tricks to keep the party going include:

♦ Allowing guests to change into their disco outfits, and you changing into something fabulous and glitzy.

♦ Asking for a fancy-dress theme in the evening, even if it means you hiring out cowboy and Indian outfits for everyone. Keep spending down by just borrowing head-dresses and hats.

♦ Open up new rooms after the formal sit-down dinner. Announce new locations to keep interest up, such as a casino, chill-out room, or a maze in the garden.

♦ Put on a show. If you don't fancy getting all theatrical, hire a local dance troupe or comedian to do it.

♦ Send off the photographer's assistant to develop the film shot earlier in the day, and set up a booth for guests to buy images, or give them tickets to get one free.

♦ Get the DJ to make special announcements, call people up to mix some tunes, hand out instruments and cos-tumes, and make jokes.

SARAH, 31

❝ Weddings can be so formulaic and I wanted ours to be as different as possible. When I got engaged, I really wanted to do something special for my husband, so I concocted a plan with my bridesmaid that I would record a song and play it as a surprise for our first dance. My husband loves the Nina Simone classic 'My Baby Just Cares for Me'. I bought one of the sophisticated backing tracks that you can get and practised secretly in my car without him knowing. I was lucky to have a friend who has a recording suite in his house who agreed to: a) get me drunk, and b) record my warbling. You can hire recording studios where they can turn you into Mariah Carey if you really want to, but I decided that I wanted my song to be 'warts and all'. At the reception, they put the song on and we danced away without him knowing that anything was amiss. I told him that it was me, and he couldn't believe it – and insisted on playing it again and again. ❞

I'll do you a favour

Everyone loves a keepsake to remind them of the good things in life – and you can't get much better than good friends getting hitched. Here are a few inventive ideas:

1. Women love things that can fit in their handbag – why not give the girls a commemorative compact mirror or packet of hankies?

2. Serve the food on a take-home place mat – or even plate – and provide a box for it to travel in. Inscribe it with a favourite joke or funny message.

3. Send your guests home with biscuits or cakes that have been decorated with pictures of you – on edible paper of course!

4. Serve an unusual aperitif – such as the Italians' favourite, Limonata – in a cool or old-fashioned bottle, with a personalised 'Cheers!' message tied around the neck.

5. Print up basketball caps or footballs with the date on for the boys.

6. Do a Homer, and leave a box of doughnuts on each seat; guests will be grateful for them on the way home. Krispy Kremes make romantic versions with pink and red sprinkles.

7. Leave a carefully written note on each seat saying that you have donated a set amount to your favourite charity instead of splashing out on wedding favours. Guests will appreciate this – and what a lovely thing to do: give back for your great day!

8. If you can't afford to leave everyone gifts, women will be more appreciative than men – who seem more than happy with a free meal and a disco. So go girlie and give the ladies a brooch or bracelet in a pretty box.

Goodie bags

Receiving a take-home gift at the end of a party takes people back to happy days of childhood, when all you needed was a slice of cake, a balloon and a toy to make your week perfect. Many couples are now copying this for their weddings, and sending guests off into the night with presents. My husband and I often stagger into hotel rooms and waiting cars clutching wonderful goodies and wearing multi-coloured decorations, singing, 'What a bloody good bash!' It really finishes the day on the right note – and helps guests through their hangovers the next morning (especially if they are sent on their way with some snacks!)

FAB IDEAS FOR GOODIE BAGS

1. A hangover pack: an eye-cooling mask, some headache tablets, a can of fizzy pop, some relaxing bath bubbles and a fast-food voucher.

2. A remember-our-day pack: personalised golf tees, soaps, notepads and pens.

3. A relaxing pack: rejuvenating face cream, bath oils and candles.

4. A CD in a commemorative case, perhaps one for the boys and one for the girls so that couples don't double up. We did this: Dean Martin for the boys and Frank Sinatra for the girls. People still play them and think of us.

5. A sweetie bag: sugar and spice and all things nice (it will probably get eaten in the cab on the way home, but the gesture was there!).

6. An 'I was there' T-shirt: 'I went to Bob and Babs' wedding and all I got ...'

7. An engraved silver photo frame or album is a lovely – if pricey – gift. Hopefully they'll put a great picture of your wedding in it.

Secrets of Success

- Instead of plain old confetti or rose peta... hand out streamers in the colour of y... purple looks particularly good. They add a ... Eve feel to your day. If you do want confetti, make your own cones. Ask your ushers to hand them to guests, or leave them at each exit. Use thick paper and double-sided tape, and decorate with ribbon in your bridesmaids' colours.

- Give all your female guests a corsage to wear; this will look pretty and make everyone feel included and special.

- On each table, make sure the decorations are low enough or high enough for guests to talk comfortably to each other. Hanging baskets attached to the ceiling as centrepieces over each table are amazing.

- If you're having a country wedding, seat guests on bails of hay covered in a protective, yet pretty, fabric.

- Fruit can make a stunningly colourful centrepiece. Use exotic fruits stacked high to pretty-up the place – and to eat. And stick tiny flags showing guests' names in as place markers.

- Ask a recommended baker and icer to make edible replicas of your wedding shoe or tiara as a special table touch.

- Leave love notes and famous sayings dotted around each table and make placemats out of your favourite pictures.

- Give different wedding favours and set different place markers for male and female guests. Packets of seeds, cacti or bulbs make long-lasting favours, as are sachets of herbs. If you have cash to splash, get wedding favours in each guest's birthstone. Just ask them to RSVP with their birthday – that'll get them guessing.

write poems for each guest – if you're having a small wedding – and leave as joint place markers and favours. They will be treasured (and they're cheap!).

◆ Instead of leaving each guest's name on the table, tie it to the relevant wine glass. This is unusual – and means they won't lose their drink! Wrap a bottle of champagne in ribbon and paper as a centrepiece, and then use it as the prize for a competition you set for each table. Put a mini-fridge on or under each table so that guests can keep their drinks cool – and offer them the chance to win it by doing a dare.

◆ If you can't afford individual favours, leave a big bowl of sweets in the centre of each table, labelled 'Sweet treats for all!'

◆ Combine two favourite modern wedding favours, by placing a lottery ticket in a fortune cookie. I recently attended a wedding where they did this, and it worked as a double treat – and a real surprise!

◆ Give out CDs of your first dance and service music as favours.

◆ If you're having a garden wedding, serve vegetables, fruit and herbs fresh from your location – and tell the guests. This is a lovely touch.

◆ After the food is served, clear an area for a mini-casino. Instead of dealing in hard cash, offer cocktails, gifts, challenges. Set up a fortune teller's booth in a quiet corner so that your friends can learn when their prince will come. Invite a tattooist to come along and decorate your guests' limbs – semi-permanently, of course. Get a face painter for the kids and dafter adults.

◆ Make your exit like a true movie star: ask for fireworks, flashing lights, and hand party poppers and streamers to guests as they bid you farewell.

Chapter Ten

The grand finale

S O MUCH ENERGY AND ENTHUSIASM goes into planning the actual 24 hours of your wedding day that the other things adding to the whole bridal experience get forgotten. Not here! This chapter will fill you in on the best gifts, honeymoons … and how to handle becoming a Mrs with style!

Get with the gift list

One of the exciting things to look forward to after the great day is opening your presents. As you are an organised bride, you will probably have arranged for a gift list to be held at a store. But which list should you go for?

1. Is the range of goods available wide, and in all price ranges?

2. Will your list be accessible by phone and the Internet?

3. Will you be sent regular updates?

4. How long it will take for goods to be delivered?

5. Is there a delivery charge for your guests?

6. Do they offer a wrapping service, and clearly mark who each gift is from?

If you have a home full of toasters, white china and alarm clocks already, here are some more unusual ideas for gifts:

◆ Ask for a tree to plant in your garden.

◆ Gourmet gifts such as popcorn machines, ice-cream makers and fondue sets are fun.

◆ Get a customised board game. Monopoly and Trivial Pursuit are available like this.

◆ Adopt an animal.

◆ Get a star named after you.

◆ First edition books will become family heirlooms.

◆ Personalised number plates can be reasonably priced.

◆ Personalised linen sets (with your new married name embroidered on them).

◆ Commission a friend to paint a picture for you.

- Ask for favourite pictures to be printed onto coasters, mats and pillowcases.

- Stock up your cellar with some fine wines.

- Get fit with some fitness machines and bicycles.

- Ask someone to order you flowers every month for a year.

- Magazine subscriptions are the gifts that keep on giving.

- Friends could club together to buy you a post-wedding-trauma weekend away.

- Ask for a donation to a charity on your behalf.

- Get your friends to club together to buy you a pet and equipment.

SADIE, 30

❝ My husband and I had shared a home for over five years so there was really very little we needed in the toaster/spoons/towels department. So we decided to be cheeky and ask friends for cash. We'd seen the cutest red MG on Ebay but couldn't afford it because the wedding was costing us so much. We were gutted – we had always fantasised about cruising country lanes in a classic soft-top. Our friends and family gave generously, and as soon as another one came up for auction it was ours. Every time I turn the key I think of our wonderful guests! ❞

Happy holiday

Just when you thought you'd peaked and it was all down-hill from now on, here comes the honeymoon – a chance to chill out, catch up on sleep and discuss the wedding with the star of the show: your new husband. So what are your options?

Home from home

The latest trend in modern honeymoons is *not* to fly away somewhere exotic, but to stay at home and spend all the cash on a few nights in the ultimate hotel. Two couples I know have done this recently to great effect. Instead of delays, airplane food and mosquito bites, they drove an hour or two to a spa that all their friends had heard of and dreamt of visiting, and indulged in early nights, massages, fantastic food and a great wine list. Don't feel you have to go a thousand miles away to have a good break. The sign of a fabulous honeymoon is how many memories you have from it, and how happy you are to relax with your groom.

Honey-commune

Another trend in honeymoons is to invite your most fun friends along for the ride. Think about it – it makes sense. The boys can get up early and play golf while you and your bezzie buddies can head to the spa for a gossip. Evenings can be spent as couples, if you wish, before meeting up for a nightcap at an agreed location. But do remember: holiday-ing *à deux* gives you more opportunity to chill out, snog and talk endlessly about how your wedding was the best ever. Group holidays can be stressful because everyone wants to spend their money and spare time in different ways.

WEATHER, GIRLS!

Some boring things need to be considered when booking your foreign honeymoon. Most important of all is what the weather will be like at the time you are planning to go. Here is a mini-global guide to maximum sunshine and minimal rain:

Spring: Jordan, Dubai, Cyprus, California, Morocco, Mauritius

Summer: New England, Italy, Sardinia, Greece and the Greek Islands

Autumn: Sri Lanka, Barbados, Brazil, Mexico, Peru, Tenerife

Winter: South Africa, St Lucia, Hawaii, the Maldives

What kind of honeymooners are you?

Don't do anything too bizarre or dangerous on your honeymoon, just because it's your honeymoon (and I'm not only talking about in the bedroom). If you've never been tempted to climb Machu Picchu or swim with sharks before, don't pick your post-wedding to do it in a bid to make your honeymoon 'special'. It will be special anyway, so do something that suits you and your bloke. Read below to see what kind of trip might be best:

Culture vultures

Grab your restaurant guide, a map and your sunglasses to see the sights in style. Who said being a tourist was unromantic? The world is full of monuments to love and museums filled with (erotic) art. If you fancy this, head to these sights for sore eyes: Venice, Verona and Florence are all perfect; India's Taj Mahal is possibly the world's greatest monument to love; Paris is eternal; Budapest, Reykjavik and Vienna have an icy charm; Marrakesh is hot and spicy.

Fun 'n' Frolics

Just because you're married, you don't have to get all mature and sensible suddenly. Far from it! True love can put a spring in your step and make you feel 17 again, so do the tackiest, silliest, funniest things you've ever wanted to. If you fancy some fun in the sun, head to: Orlando for a meeting with Mickey and Minnie; Dubai to make a big splash at Wild Wadi Waterpark; Las Vegas for a flutter in fantasy land; Ibiza for the 24-hour clubbing and foam parties; and Rio de Janeiro for Caipirinhas and carnivals.

Sweetheart skiing

Hitting slopes doesn't have to mean aching muscles and dodgy tan lines! Oh no, pick the resort carefully, and the snow and sunshine can only make for an unforgettable honeymoon in the mountains. Who needs tropical beaches? If you fancy this, slope off to these romantic resorts: Aspen, Banff, Gstaad, Klosters, Meribel, Livigno, St Moritz or Whistler.

Safari so good

Get animal in the outback! Just imagine all those hippos rolling in mud (after all, there's nothing quite like it for soothing the blood). What could be more invigorating than waking at sunrise to head out into the open plain to see giraffes, elephants and tigers? Try Kenya, Sun City in South Africa, Mozambique – or do an elephant safari in Sri Lanka, or see the monkeys in Borneo.

Sea world

If the kind of world you want to see is under the sea, don't settle for a few passing mackerel and a grumpy conger eel.

You need to find your own Atlantis, and a school where you can take your diving exams if you haven't already. For turtles, fly to Tenerife. For sharks, go to South Africa. For tropical fish, go to the Indian Ocean or Red Sea, and for crustaceans, head out to the Florida Keys.

> **NB Bride's head revisited!** Why not go back to the place you and your groom most love in the world. There are no rules stating you have to go somewhere unexplored on your honeymoon. If your first weekend away together as a couple was perfect, re-live it. Or go where your parents or in-laws went on their honeymoon and report back on how it has changed.

Go bespoke

If you're not sure what you want to do, get someone else to free your mind. Contact a travel specialist, or even write to the travel desk of a newspaper with your dilemmas and queries. The world is getting smaller and smaller, and there are very few places (depending on your budget!) that you can't go to for a bit of romance.

> **JILL, 40**
>
> ❝ We followed Route 66 and it was amazing – quite unlike honeymoons that our other friends had embarked on. Instead of smooching at sunset, we met cowboys and celebrities, drove through desert and vineyards, went to film premieres and book-signings. It was exhausting, but very 'us'. It felt like we'd had a year away from our normal lives rather than just three weeks. ❞

Travel 'in' packs

Cool things to shove in your suitcase for a blissful honeymoon include:

◆ An iPod with all your wedding tunes on.

◆ At least one wedding photo to show to other honeymooners.

◆ Plenty of non-wedding-related reading material.

◆ Edible chocolate body paint.

◆ Sequined, bow-tie knickers (too impractical for normal days!).

◆ A portable DVD player for early nights in bed.

◆ This book and a pen, so you can tick off all the amazing things you did at your wedding!

The morning after the night before

So your wedding day is over, and there's just the honeymoon to look forward to. Right? Wrong! First of all, don't get depressed. Yes, the 'big day' is over, but the rest of your uniquely wonderful life as a married woman has just begun. And what better way to begin a life of wedded bliss than with a honeymoon to inspire envy in close friends and a lifetime of memorable, er, memories for you and your beloved? But before you fly off, take a leaf out of many a modern bride's notebook, and continue the celebrations for your nearest and dearest into the next day.

Over 100 of our friends and family stayed at the hotel where we got married, so we had a celebratory full English breakfast together, six hours after the official party had finished at 3.00 a.m. Despite being more tired than I had ever been in my life (and having feet the size of lifeboats after an evening of wild-banshee dancing), it was fun to get up and share our hangover hell, swap snogging gossip and open presents in front of the people who gave them to us. So do think about staying in the same hotel as your guests, rather than buggering off for a romantic night, which will probably never happen, as you'll be too busy sleeping/aching/talking/puking (delete as appropriate).

Other friends have continued the party the day after by:

♦ Hosting a cocktail party at their home to show off their gifts.

♦ Holding a wedding video screening at a suitable location.

♦ Asking their parents to host a BBQ, if the weather was suitable.

♦ Inviting close friends to join them for the first few days of the honeymoon.

♦ Booking a table at their favourite local restaurant to thank helpers.

♦ Taking the parents and in-laws out for a five-star 'getting to know you' lunch.

♦ Doing a driving tour of the guests who live locally, collecting memories and good-luck wishes.

♦ Hosting a 'breakfast in bed' in the honeymoon suite for the A-list.

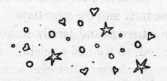

NB When to leave your own wedding? Making an elegant exit at the reception says cool and sophisticated. Leaving the day after makes sense: minimum holiday wastage from work. The day that allows you to get together with friends and family and get your fill of gossip and glamour before you leave for your holiday. If you're not going on honeymoon, enlist a friend to fill your home with everything you need so that you can hide away for a few days (the latest CDs and DVDs, a gourmet hamper, pampering products and fresh flowers). And then don't answer the phone. Not even to your mother. And especially not to your mother-in-law.

The after effects

The wedding may officially be over but with a little carefully placed genius, no one will ever forget it – and they will think fondly of you and your big day forever.

◆ Send guests off with something they can keep and treasure, even if it's just a laminated place mat with their name and your wedding date on.

◆ Post thank-you cards, specially printed with a photograph on the cover of you taking your vows, or enclose a picture in their card of you with them on the great day.

◆ Invite close friends and family round for a video evening.

◆ Take the immediate wedding party out for a 'reunion' dinner at the reception venue when you return from honeymoon.

- Get a web-friendly friend to set up an Internet site full of pictures, where guests can post their post-wedding stories and gossip while you're away. You can log on when you're fed up with sightseeing or sunbathing.

- Contact the local paper or a wedding magazine to run a feature about your wedding.

- Arrange for the cloakroom attendants to put thank-you notes or little gifts in everyone's coat pocket before they leave.

- If most of your guests are staying in the hotel where you held the reception, arrange for the housekeeping staff to leave 'Good night, sleep tight' messages under their pillows and spray some relaxing lavender scent on their duvets.

- If you have one special, single girlfriend who you'd like to have your bouquet, don't throw it during the reception, but have it sent to her the morning after the wedding.

Thank you, thank you, thank you

How to thank those who've helped you over the most joyfully stressful months of your life doesn't have to be difficult or expensive – in fact, it can be fun!

So the normal thing is to give the mothers flowers and the fathers a firm handshake. Dull, dull, dull! And mothers being mothers, they only worry about how they are going to get the bouquets home safely! The year I got married, I'd paid careful attention to what our wedding party were into. I bought the mothers beautiful (yet not expensive) handbags from a high street store and I bought the fathers books and games related to their current interests. These were easy to store, easy to wrap and made the recipients very happy. What more can you ask for? Other great ideas include jewellery, photo albums and frames, hotel reservations (so that they can relax while you're relaxing on your honeymoon), and beauty treatment vouchers. Basically, any luxury that they would not treat themselves to will go down very well indeed.

Amazing anniversaries

So, your year of being a bride is coming to the end. The grand finale should be a wonderful night celebrating your first year of being Mrs Wife. You could:

◆ Return to where he/you proposed with a bottle of champers.

◆ Go for dinner where you had your reception and have the wedding breakfast again.

◆ Hold a wedding video evening at your house.

◆ Hire the wedding DJ or band for a party at your local pub/bar.

◆ Take your parents out for a slap-up meal.

◆ Have a big buffet do at your house to show off the gifts you received a year ago on your wedding registry!

And not forgetting gifts for you and your groom, here's the traditional guide, which can be uniquely adapted to your own personalities:

◆ The first is PAPER, so buy theatre or plane tickets and book hotel rooms.

- The second is COTTON, so indulge in new sheets, or a new wardrobe.

- The third is LEATHER, so think shoes, handbags, watches and luggage.

- The fourth is BOOKS, so go for a first edition or a signed tome.

- The fifth is WOOD, so what about garden furniture or a croquet set?

After a few years of marriage, what you want on your anniversary becomes a whole lot clearer:

- Twenty-fifth is SILVER

- Thirtieth is PEARL

- Thirty-fifth is CORAL

- Fortieth is RUBY

- Forty-fifth is SAPPHIRE

- Fiftieth is GOLDEN

- Fifty-fifth is EMERALD

- Sixtieth is DIAMOND

- Sixty-fifth is BLUE SAPPHIRE

- Seventieth is PLATINUM

- Seventy-fifth is DIAMOND AND GOLD – a bumper year, if you make it that far!

FOR EVER

Another modern way to celebrate your love – of your husband and presents – is for your man to buy you an eternity ring, be it on your first anniversary or the birth of your first child. As this ring is a celebration of what makes you such a wonderful wife (and person, of course), choose a ring in your birth stone:

January: garnet	July: ruby
February: amethyst	August: peridot
March: aquamarine	September: sapphire
April: diamond	October: opal
May: emerald	November: topaz
June: pearl	December: turquoise

Final destination

So you've had your unique wedding, it was the best day of your life and you've got the pictures to prove it. Now you just have to work on the marriage – and this is where the hard work starts. Planning a unique and wonderful wedding is easy compared to maintaining a happy relationship. There'll be tears, traumas and tantrums – and marriage does change your relationship more than you imagine it could, from the inside and to the outside world. But it can be worth it. Just try to remember all the uniquely special things about your new husband, understand that no relationship is perfect, and be prepared to work hard. You'll

be all right. Good luck – I wish you many, many years of
married bliss!

Secrets of Success

♦ Feeling depressed that you'll never get to wear your wedding
garb ever again? Don't panic. A friend recently told me about
her depressed ex-bride mate who decided to hold wedding-
dress parties for all the girls in her life who felt the same way.
So once a year, the men don black tie and the girls put on
their frocks. Now that's a dinner party with a difference.

♦ Another way to stop feeling your outfit is dead and buried is
to offer elements of it to your mates who are about to get
hitched – even if it's just the tiara, or a funny suspender belt,
or the veil. It will be a good way to cover the something old,
something new, something borrowed, something blue – and
help her save some cash.

♦ While we're on the subject, if you *really* loved your dress, and
you feel it is of a classically stylish nature, make sure you pre-
serve it carefully. Get the professionals in to help. Your
daughter may wear it one day (although you must not put
any pressure on her to do so when you become a pushy
mother of the bride!).

♦ If your wedding was a great success – and no one has
stopped talking about it months after the event – how about
hiring a screening room in a local cinema and showing your
video for your first anniversary celebrations. Make sure it's
good quality – no flashing or wobbly sections – then invite
your friends and family, and pop the bubbly once again.

♦ Don't expect your honeymoon to be all moonlight and roses.
You'll be tired, deflated, and weirded-out. Don't feel like a

failure if you have an argument. There's nothing unique about squabbling honeymooners at all.

◆ Make sure your honeymoon isn't memorable for the wrong reasons. However rushed you are coping with the wedding, don't forget to pack properly. Remember insect repellent, high-factor sun cream, contraceptives and a first-aid kit. Perhaps put a trusted friend in charge of this, as you will be busy the week before your wedding.

◆ Don't get depressed that it's all over ... think about the holidays, parties, anniversaries, children and grandchildren that will all form the rich tapestry of your married life. There's nothing dull about all that.

Index